D0229734

I 'se for *Brilliant Selling*

B
F
Fa

A read for anyone aspiring to excel in sales.

J ·isk, *President, Outdoor & Action Sports, EMEA, VF Corporation*

Selling is very practical and accessible, without a lot of the
ou see in many sales books. Readers will get real and tangible
om this rich and informative book. I highly recommend it!

Paul Matthews, Managing Director, People Alchemy

oul l recommend this book to anyone who wants to improve
r u derstanding of the sales process and the art of developing
r laging long-term commercial relationships, which turn into
g partnerships.

Philip Jansen, Chief Executive, Sodexo Europe

selling

What the best salespeople know, do and say

Jeremy Cassell
Tom Bird

Harlow, England • London • New York • Boston • San Francisco • Toronto • Sydney • Singapore • Hong Kong
Tokyo • Seoul • Taipei • New Delhi • Cape Town • Madrid • Mexico City • Amsterdam • Munich • Paris • Milan

PEARSON EDUCATION LIMITED

Edinburgh Gate
Harlow CM20 2JE
Tel: +44 (0)1279 623623
Fax: +44 (0)1279 431059
Website: www.pearsoned.co.uk

First published in Great Britain in 2009

© Pearson Education 2009

The rights of Jeremy Cassell and Tom Bird to be identified as authors of this work has been asserted by them in accordance with the Copyright, Designs and Patents Act 1988.

ISBN: 978-0-273-72646-3

British Library Cataloguing-in-Publication Data
A catalogue record for this book is available from the British Library

Library of Congress Cataloging-in-Publication Data
A catalog record for this book is available from the Library of Congress

10 9 8 7 6 5 4 3 2 1
13 12 11 10 09

Cartoons by Sarah Arnold
Typeset in 10/14pt Plantin by 30
Printed in Great Britain by Henry Ling Ltd., at the Dorset Press, Dorchester, Dorset

The publisher's policy is to use paper manufactured from sustainable forests.

Contents

About the authors

Jeremy Cassell: I started out as a teacher when I left university. I taught English to A level, History to GCSE, ran the hockey club, coached other sports and ended up as Head of Drama at Kelly College in Devon.

After a brief spell in commercial finance, I started my formal selling career in a classic FMCG role – as a territory salesman for L'Oreal. I doubled the sales turnover in three years and even won a new Mini in a generous sales promotion! I ended up as Head of Training and Development focusing on developing the sales force.

After a brief spell at Pepsi and a management consultancy, I ended up doing what I always wanted to do – being my own boss! RTP (**www.rtpc.co.uk**) was established in 1999 and a few years later Tom Bird joined. RTP is a performance improvement consultancy.

So, I have been involved in selling learning, drama, hair products, crisps, consultancy, training and coaching.

I am TEFL-qualified, a certified coach and an NLP (Neuro-Linguistic Programming) trainer. I work in professional service firms, large organisations and SMEs, delivering training and coaching around all areas of influencing and communication.

Outside work I play and watch a lot of sport, collect second-hand books and love spending time with my partner Nicky and our three kids (Felix, Benjamin and Isabella) who are learning how to sell all the time!

Tom Bird: I enjoyed a 15-year career in sales and business management before becoming a full-time consultant, trainer and coach. I'd like to say that the move into sales was strategic and the result of careful consideration, but in fact it was because British Airways didn't want to take someone with my poor eyesight and lack of qualifications to fly 747s (my original dream!).

Starting as a sales executive, I cut my teeth opening new accounts for measurement systems used in petrol forecourts. I moved into high-tech and software and worked with four companies over a period of 12 years in roles including Sales Manager, Sales Director, Vice-President of European Operations and Managing Director. A number of these companies started life as privately-owned US parent companies that eventually went public on the NASDAQ. This gave me broad exposure to the different challenges of private and public companies as well as experience of sales and management in the UK, Europe and the USA.

My training, consulting and coaching work in sales is supported by a Postgraduate Diploma in Business Coaching and qualifications in Business and Finance. I am also a Master Practitioner of NLP.

Outside of my work I am passionate about music (in which I have little talent), cooking (in which I have absolutely no qualifications whatsoever) and spending time with my wife Jeanette and two young children Ellie and James (both of whom give me lots of opportunities to practise and improve my sales abilities!).

How this book works

We have all bought books that we started with the best of intentions but put back on the shelf without finishing. **Brilliant Selling** is different. You do not have to read it from cover to cover. You do not have to have read and understood one chapter before you can move on to the next. You don't even have to read all the chapter content to get the key points and 'best practice' tips for that topic (although it would benefit you if you did!).

So, how can you use **Brilliant Selling** to get the information that you want in the way that you want it?

- Each chapter within the book has been written so that it stands alone. It provides useful information on the topic without you needing to have read anything else in the book.

- Every chapter has a 'Brilliant Recap' at the end. This is a bullet-point list of the key points.

- Within each chapter we have put features such as quotes, exercises and key ideas. These are highlighted so that you can go straight to them.

- You can also read **Brilliant Selling** all the way through from start to finish just like a 'normal' book of course!

However you choose to use this book, we have focused on filling it with practical, targeted information which is supplemented by additional resources at **www.brilliant-selling.com**. Just send an email to **resources@brilliant-selling.com** to receive your exclusive free resource pack, to help you make the most of this book.

Introduction

We have all bought books that we were convinced we would read but now sit on our shelf with a corner turned in around page 27. We want **Brilliant Selling** to be different.

We talked to a lot of people involved in sales about what they would find useful and how they would like to use a book on the subject. We created a specific sales survey in which we asked over 200 successful salespeople how they sell effectively. We have used a fair amount of the evidence from this survey in the book. More can be found on our website – www.brilliant-selling.com.

We recognise that you may have some very specific questions about selling. These may include:

- What specifically can I do to improve my performance immediately?
- How can I sell well in an economic downturn?
- How can I make more money?
- What is current 'Best Practice' in selling?

With many years of sales experience behind us, we thought you would appreciate lots of academic theoretical models, impenetrable data and detailed case studies that do not relate at all to your market ... Maybe not! We want to focus on what works in selling. How about a book full of practical tips, war stories and exercises, based on best practice that is guaranteed to improve your results? Would that hit the spot?

We have written **Brilliant Selling** for people like you, who 'touch' selling in different ways. So, who are you?

- You work for a small or medium sized company where everyone needs to have a basic grasp of how to sell effectively and interact with customers.
- You are on the periphery of sales – perhaps in a support function that touches sales, and need an understanding of the process and priorities.
- You are either new to sales or experienced in selling and want to benchmark yourself against current 'best practice'.
- You are involved in maximising sales performance in some way – perhaps as a sales manager, sales trainer, consultant or coach.
- You may have 'fallen into' selling accidentally but recognise it is important as you develop your business or career.

You may also be selling to different types of customer in different markets and in different ways...

- 'Business to Business' or 'Business to Consumer'.
- Selling a product or service – commodity or bespoke.
- Selling directly to end-users or via a distribution network.
- Selling face-to-face, online, via the telephone or some combination of these.

Whoever you are, we believe **Brilliant Selling** can help.

Who are we to write about selling?

Neither of us studied hard at school or university with the express desire of becoming salespeople. We did not dream of our perfect company car, the cut and thrust of sales meetings with customers or the feeling of euphoria that comes with achieving a sale against the odds. We are both 'accidental' salesmen. We found ourselves in sales-related roles as much through a quirky set of circumstances as from a conscious choice.

Our sales careers have been a lot of things: enjoyable, challenging, frustrating, rewarding and, perhaps above all, self-taught. We got into sales via circuitous routes and proceeded to navigate our way through a career that was largely based on developing our own ideas of how to sell effectively. Yes, there were sales courses we attended which were helpful, but there was nothing that provided a straightforward and complete picture of what selling was and how to do it well.

Even many years into our careers there were still questions in our minds:

- 'Am I doing this right?'
- 'Am I missing something?'
- 'Is what I am doing "good practice"?'

Do you share these concerns? Our intention is that **Brilliant Selling** will answer these questions for you!

What is in the book and how should I use it?

There are six sections, each with key specific chapters focused on different elements of selling.

The six sections are:

1 **You**
   This is about you as an individual and how your personality, beliefs, values and habits impact on your sales performance. It will help you identify where to focus your efforts to improve performance.

2 **Process and planning**

It may not be why you enjoy sales but the sales process and your own planning can be critical to consistency and improved performance. We give you the key priorities.

3 **Your power to influence**

How do you build credible relationships where you can influence, communicate and negotiate with confidence? What are the core skills you need and how do you develop them?

4 **Understanding buyers and prospects**

The inside track on identifying the motivations of buyers and prospects, getting the appointment and what to do in the first meeting.

5 **Presenting solutions**

Focuses on how to get the sales result that you want from a compelling sales proposal and a persuasive sales presentation. The chapter will also demonstrate how to meet objections and gain agreement.

6 **Developing customers**

Once you have the sale, how do you manage customers to develop the relationship and sell more to them?

Not everyone wants to read a book from start to finish. You may have some specific questions that relate to one of the main sections of the book. Therefore, you can read any section that you want in whatever order you want. Simply 'dip in and out' of the book as defined by your needs or interests. We have, however, structured the sections in a logical order should you want to start at the front!

To make **Brilliant Selling** even more practical and easy for you to consume, we have included the following features:

● Brilliant Tips: Key information is summarised in the form of bullet points, making it quick and easy for you to pick up the information that will make a difference to your performance.

- War Stories: Stories help bring techniques to life and show you how they can be applied in the real world, speeding up your understanding and application.

- Exercises: Each section has exercises that you can complete for yourself. This brings the content of this book right into your world, to help you achieve the results you want.

By purchasing this book you also have free access to the **www.brilliant-selling.com** website, which provides you with more top tips and additional free resources to continue your own personal sales development. This website includes an analysis of a sales survey which was completed by over 200 successful sales people from across many markets. All you need to do is send an email to: **resources@brilliant-selling.com** to receive your exclusive free resource pack.

Before you read on...

Think about your goals for reading this book. What do you want to achieve specifically? What difference would it make to your job, your career and your financial success if you were even better at just one of the aspects of selling that are addressed by this book?

What if you could increase your performance as it relates to selling by even 10% or 15%? What sort of impact would that have? You can start right away ... and please, get past page 27!

PART 1

You

Have you ever surprised yourself by achieving something that you thought unlikely or even impossible?

A couple of years back I found myself in a sales situation, in which I felt increasingly pessimistic about securing the order. The value of the deal was high; the competition was known to me and strong – we were the underdogs. I found myself thinking more and more about times in the past when I had lost to this competitor and 'wasted' a lot of time in the process. I finally plucked up the courage to go to my sales director and come clean about my concerns. After listening to me, he simply asked me a couple of key questions:

'Do you believe that we have the best solution for this prospect's needs?' and 'Have you asked the prospect where they see us being able to add most value to them?'

Two simple and appropriate questions that forced me to think.

I began to realise that I was losing sight of the most important thing in this deal – the value I could add and the perception of me in the eyes of the prospect. What I had done was follow a pattern that had been holding me back from winning deals above a certain value, especially when I was competing with this one specific competitor. Whenever I got an opportunity like this one, I seemed to follow the same pattern of thinking, which then impacted my behaviour. What my sales director had done was raise my own awareness of this and encourage me to focus on the right things and, in doing so, to question those barriers to success that were really holding me back!

If you think about the typical salesperson, what comes to mind? A lot of people conjure up a picture of a particular type of person that they associate with a selling role. This section will answer questions including:

- Do I have the right personality to sell?
- Are there specific aspects of my personality that support or detract from my performance?
- How do my beliefs impact on my results for good or bad?
- What should I focus on if I want to improve continually?

What if you could become consciously aware of the beliefs that hold you back and do something about them? What if you could change your habitual way of communicating to more closely meet how the other person prefers to take in information? What sort of impact would that have?

CHAPTER 1

The personality of a salesperson

Personality plays a big part in becoming a brilliant salesperson but there are a couple of additional 'truths' of which you may not be consciously aware:

1 There is no one 'right' personality for a Brilliant Salesperson – there are introvert and extrovert salespeople, technical and non-technical.

2 You may not yet be aware of the aspects of your own personality that support or detract from the sales results you achieve.

Each of us has a number of different 'personalities' that we use in different situations. We might be very different when we are alone, compared with when we are with our friends, and different again with our family or when we are at work. Are you aware of what characterises your selling personality? How do you think, act and behave when you are in the selling role?

Brilliant salespeople do focus consciously on their personality. They identify what works and do more of it and they identify what about their personality holds them back and they change it.

'We are what we repeatedly do. Excellence, then, is not an act, but a habit' – Aristotle

Be aware of your sales persona

🡒 **brilliant** exercise

Think for a moment about when you last bought something of value. In addition to your desire to purchase the item, what convinced you to buy? What did you appreciate about **how** you were sold to?

Now think about a time when you wanted to buy something but chose not to because you did not like the approach of the salesperson. What was it, specifically, that you did not like?

Finally, write down five words that describe the personality of your 'ideal' salesperson – a person most likely to make the sale to you.

Are you conscious?

When we approach selling we often do not think consciously about how we are going to do it and whether this approach will help or hinder our success. We are processing so much information every second of every day that we simply have to adopt habits. Over time, these habits become unconscious – we do them without thinking.

Everyone sells differently and we need to be ourselves to sell authentically. It is no good trying to 'become' someone else when we sell. What we need to do is to consciously understand ourself and our preferences, or habits, so that we can do more of what works and change what does not whilst still being ourself! We have lots of different preferences that determine what we pay attention to, what motivates us and how we respond in a given situation.

Before we look at specific preferences let us think about how we learn and improve.

When we learn something, we go through a period of time when we have to put all of our attention on the thing we are learning – for example riding a bicycle. After a while, this simply becomes an unconscious skill. We have developed a habit.

> To create or change a habit we need three things: knowledge, desire and awareness.

To create or change a habit we need three things: knowledge, desire and awareness.

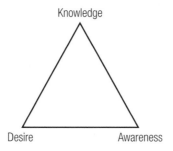

Knowledge

Desire   Awareness

We need to be consciously aware of our existing habits if we are to change them. We need to have the knowledge of how to change (this book will help you there!) and we must have the real desire to make that change now. Some of our selling habits already support a good result and we need to be aware of these as well. The more consciously competent we are at some aspect of selling, the better we will get at it.

What are some important preferences?

Listed below are some preferences that will impact (often unconsciously) our approach to selling. Of course, our prospects and customers will also have preferences and we will look at these in more detail in Part 3 of this book. Each preference is shown as a set of two extremes but personality is not as clear as that. Consider each as a spectrum with you sitting somewhere on the line between the two extremes. Some of these preferences depend on context, and so think about them relative to your selling role.

This is by no means an exhaustive list of preferences – we have just chosen three for you to consider and raise your awareness as to how they will impact on how you approach selling. As you review these three preferences, think about where you sit on the line and how these preferences influence your selling style. There are no 'rights and wrongs' to these preferences. However, being aware of yours will help you **choose** how to respond more effectively.

1 **Do we take action or do we reflect?**

Action   Reflector

How do you approach building a new piece of flat-pack furniture that you have bought? Do you open the box and immediately start to construct it or do you prefer to read the instructions first, maybe laying out the pieces and thinking how you will approach the task? Imagine having a strong 'action oriented' approach to your selling role. You are probably great at picking up the phone, arranging meetings and following through on actions.

But what about the planning aspects? Maybe you pick up the phone but have not truly thought through the right approach to take with the call. If you prefer to reflect, you are probably fantastic at thinking things through before you act. But do you put off action too long as a result? Maybe you have a very well thought out plan but do not always follow-through on the calls, meetings and visits necessary to turn it into success. As a person with an 'Action' preference, I know that I have learnt to be more reflective and this has helped my selling significantly. Where I used to turn up to meetings and 'wing it' I now have thought through an agenda and the possible issues that will arise.

	Action oriented	Reflector
Strengths	You make things happen Self-starter Want to implement Seen by others as having 'energy' Do not avoid action	Take time planning and thinking things through Consider the 'right' approach taking account of all the issues Gain lots of information through your conversations
Warnings	You may not always plan thoroughly Can be accused of 'acting first, thinking later' May irritate 'reflector' oriented prospects May not uncover needs as effectively as a 'reflector'	May over-analyse at the expense of action Could irritate 'action' oriented prospects May miss opportunities that are time-bound

tips

If you are action-oriented, make an effort to pay attention to those aspects of selling that you might rush. They are likely to include planning for meetings, considering all the options before you propose something or take action, and being extra-aware of those prospects who may be reflectors.

If you are more reflective, think about when you need to move into an action-oriented phase. Be aware of the need to take decisions with imperfect information and be especially aware when you are selling to people who are action-oriented.

2 Do we prefer detail or big picture?

Big picture   Detail

How much information do you need to feel comfortable with completing a task? Do you set headline goals or are you better at breaking these down into specific milestones?

Big picture people prefer scope to depth. They often give an overview without the detail. I had a sales manager once who communicated a new sales strategy to me by giving me the big picture and he was completely unaware that I needed more detail – it simply was not important to him. Detail people, by contrast, prefer depth to scope. They are more comfortable with having more information about a given task. They might notice small inconsistencies that simply would not interest a big picture person. This preference can come across in both written and verbal communication and we would do well to understand better the needs of the person with whom we are communicating. If we simply give a big picture overview they may be left wanting more detail.

If we go into small detail we may be frustrating the other person, who might merely want an overview.

The easiest thing to do is to ask how much information a person needs. If you are writing a proposal, this would be a useful thing to do! I have, in the past, sent a proposal with page after page of information and detail to someone who simply wanted a summary and some bullet points.

	Big picture	Detail
Strengths	Puts things in perspective – keeps the bigger picture in mind Can see how things link together Good at giving an overview	Pays attention to important detail Comprehensive and complete in approach and correspondence
Warnings	Can irritate detail-conscious people May be seen as not paying attention to important detail May leave some important information out of proposals and other communications	May pay attention to unimportant detail Can irritate a big-picture person with too much information May not 'see the wood for the trees' and could focus on the wrong things

brilliant tips

If you are a big-picture person, remember that some people need more information. Think about those aspects of your selling work that would benefit from a more detailed focus. These might include proposals and presentations. If you are presenting, make sure you have more detail in handouts.

If you are a detail-conscious person, make sure you pay attention to the right details. Ensure you can summarise your messages and think about using diagrams to help articulate complex ideas.

> In both instances, notice what the other person needs in terms of detail. You can always ask them: 'How much detail do you need from me?'

3   **Are we motivated towards something we want or away from something we do not want?**

Away from   Towards

I realised, after 10 years in a variety of jobs, that I made a decision to move on, not because the new job was what I really wanted, but that it moved me away from issues and problems I was experiencing in the old job. This is very different from making choices based on knowing what you want. I went on to realise that this preference was present in a lot of decision making in which I was involved. Even if I was asked where I wanted to go to dinner by my wife I would find it easier to tell her first where I did not want to go. These are examples of 'Away From' motivation. It is not wrong; it is simply more about problem avoidance than seeking a goal.

> notice what the other person needs in terms of detail

The reverse is 'Towards' motivation. A friend of mine is intensely 'towards'. He does not think about problem avoidance at all. He simply considers what it is he wants and the outcome he is seeking.

Think about this preference in terms of selling to someone who is different from you. If I am 'Away From', I might be positioning what I can do in terms of problems that the client will avoid. This is fine if they are similar to me but if they are 'Towards' they might get frustrated at this apparent 'problem' focus. Conversely, if they are 'Away From' and I am 'Towards' they might see me as missing the point if they are looking to resolve issues and problems.

	Towards	Away From
Strengths	Can set compelling goals around desired outcomes Actions and milestones take you towards what you want rather than simply away from what you do not want	You are motivated by avoiding problems and negative consequences Can see possible pitfalls in ideas and proposals and can look at how these can be avoided or overcome
Warnings	May not see some of the potential pitfalls that you need to avoid with prospects May be seen as too goal-oriented by 'Away From' prospects	May be so motivated by problem avoidance that you are not clear on what you want instead (your desired outcome) Can be seen as 'negative' by people with a 'Towards' preference May lack clear and compelling career goals

brilliant tip

When you are setting sales and career goals for yourself, make sure they are expressed in 'Towards' terms – what is it that you really want rather than what are you looking to avoid or not have? Notice what motivates you and when you are using language that demonstrates this – are you making decisions to avoid something you do not want or to achieve something that you really want?

Brilliant recap

Knowing more about your personality will definitely improve your selling ability. This chapter has introduced some ideas that you can explore yourself:

- There is no 'right' sales personality but people all sell differently.

- Our approach, behaviours and communication are based on unconscious preferences or habits that we have developed.

- Some of these habits support our performance and others detract from it.

- To create or change a habit we need three things: knowledge, desire and awareness.

- Knowing our preferences enables us to be flexible, to adapt when we must in order to achieve the result we want.

- Always be aware that your way of communicating might be different from the person with whom you are communicating!

CHAPTER 2

How beliefs and values impact sales success

Many years ago I went in to pitch for some business at a large international bank. At the time I was new into providing consultancy and training on a self-employed basis and, whilst I felt that I provided real value, I had a limiting belief about the daily rate that I could charge. A friend of mine who arranged the introduction met me in the reception area and his words surprised me. He said, 'Don't think about charging less than £2,300 per day or you won't be taken seriously.'

What were my beliefs here?

What were the beliefs of my friend?

What were the beliefs of the organisation to which I was looking to sell?

Success in selling is due to much more than the behaviours and skills of the salesperson. Our decisions and motivations in selling are based on our beliefs and values. To a large extent they will determine our success.

What are beliefs and values and how are they formed?

Values

Our values are quite literally those things that are important to us, and we have values around most aspects of our life.

Some general values include:

Autonomy	*Creativity*	*Freedom*	*Trust*
Fun	*Responsibility*	*Money*	*Security*
Helping	*Respect*	*Fulfilment*	*Honesty*
Time Keeping	*Results*	*Recognition*	*Status*

Selling is no different, and we will have some specific values around it as well.

'Happiness is that state of consciousness that proceeds from the achievement of one's values.' – Ayn Rand

brilliant exercise

Think for a moment about the job you are doing now. Answer the question: 'What do you enjoy and value about it?' Another question to think about is: 'What's important to you about selling?' Write down a list of words that come to mind in answer to that question. These are your values around selling.

What is in your list of values around selling? It is important to pay attention to these values and sell in a way that supports them or, at the very least, does not actively work against them. If you ignore your values you are limiting your success. Remember, Brilliant Selling is about being more of who you are and your values are key. For example, if you value trust, it is likely that you look for opportunities to honour this value and this will support you in selling ethically. If you have trust as a value but work in an environment where it is impossible to live that value, then this will be the cause of frustration and concern to you.

> If you ignore your values you are limiting your success

Does money feature in your values?

The best salespeople do have money in their values. If it is important to them, they are likely naturally to take actions that support them in realising more of it! If money is not

> Brilliant Selling is about being more of who you are

in your list of values then take some time to consider why not and what is in your values that can be linked with money. Having money as a value is not wrong – it enables you to do the things that you want and you can become a money magnet!

'We can tell our values by looking at our chequebook stubs' – Gloria Steinem

Beliefs around selling and your ability to sell effectively

What are your views of a used-car salesman? My original view was that they were out to make a fast buck through smooth talking and manipulation. This view meant that for years I would not buy from independent used car showrooms. Recently I met someone who changed my belief by providing the most professional service I had ever experienced when buying any car, let alone a used car.

What do you think people believe about you when you sell to them?

What are your real beliefs about selling?

If you think selling is manipulative then you are more likely to give up at the first 'no' or objection that you receive.

Beliefs are simply those things that we feel are true and they underpin our actions. They can support our sales performance or limit it.

'To succeed we must first believe that we can' – Michael Korda

Think about this belief:

'I can't sell something that I don't believe in.'

How might this impact your performance for good or bad? The power of beliefs can be illustrated by the following example.

 example

Imagine being asked to cold call for the next two weeks. How would you feel? Some of you might look forward to the opportunity but a lot of you might be saying something like: 'I could never do that!' It is your beliefs that are driving your response. If you are saying 'I could never do that!' it is not strictly true. I mean, what would happen if you did? If cold calling was a necessary part of creating new opportunities then your belief would be limiting you. Often, if you ask someone who enjoys cold calling what they believe about it, they say things like 'It's just a numbers game,' or 'The rejection is not personal,' or even 'I think we have something of value to the prospect and I owe it to them to tell them about it'. Think about how the result you achieve is likely to be very different with these different beliefs.

Positive beliefs about selling will allow you to communicate passionately and convincingly. But if you do not believe in what you are selling this is likely to come across to the other person and you are less likely to be convincing. It is also interesting to ask yourself the question 'What makes me believe in something?' The answers are going to be linked closely with your values.

brilliant exercise

Ask yourself: 'What makes me believe in something that I am selling?'

Write down the answers. These are a checklist of qualities that are important to you. How do you rank right now against each of them? What do you need to pay attention to in your selling, based on your answers?

Do your current beliefs enable you to be passionate and convincing?

So, beliefs are not THE truth, they are just true for you. Beliefs are very personal to us – they come from friends, family, geography, and many are formed early in our lives.

'Myths which are believed in tend to become true' – George Orwell

brilliant exercise

1 Write down as many beliefs around sales and selling that you hold right now.

2 Think about the beliefs that you think the most successful salesperson you know holds.

3 Notice what the differences are, if any. What beliefs do you hold about sales and selling that are holding you back? Make a list of these.

How can you find out your beliefs around sales and selling? Well, you can simply ask yourself what you believe and write them down.

What can we do about beliefs that limit our sales success?

We now know something about beliefs. In his book *The Fifth Discipline* Peter Senge summarises William Isaacs' 'Ladder of Inference' model to describe how beliefs are formed.

At the bottom rung we observe data – we see things as they are. Because we cannot process all the data that we receive, we make unconscious selections of the data to which we will pay attention. We then add meaning to the data that we have selected and then we make assumptions based on this meaning. We then draw conclusions based on these assumptions from which our beliefs are formed. With every rung of the ladder we climb, we are moving further away from the objective 'truth'. By the time we have formed a belief, it is not really based on objective fact at all.

This is the start point for changing our limiting beliefs – they are not objectively true...

For each limiting belief, start looking for objective evidence to the contrary of the belief. For example, if you believe that 'everyone I cold call feels that I am interrupting them,' start looking for evidence that this is not true. It might be that you have managed to have useful conversations with some people as a result of cold calling or even secured an appointment. Well, for these people your belief does not seem to be true. The problem with a belief is that we often discount evidence that does not support it. We are likely to say things like 'Well, that's an exception.' It also helps for us to think about the ultimate cost of holding this limiting belief. The following exercise will help to illustrate this.

↗ brilliant exercise

Identify a belief that is limiting your sales performance now, and write it down.

For this limiting belief, really engage with the belief and what it means. Now consider what you will be doing (specifically, physically, mentally, etc.) if you are holding this limiting belief. Get really clear on this and write down as many things as you can think of. Finally, based on what you have written down in the 'Doing' step, think about what you will have as a result of doing those things. Follow the 'Doing' actions through to their result. Doing this will help you realise the ultimate cost of holding the belief.

Now think about an alternative belief that you really can hold to be true. In the cold call example, instead of believing 'everyone I cold call feels that I am interrupting them' you might be able to believe 'I have something to offer that will be of value to the people I am calling'.

▶

With this new belief, run it through the 'Belief – Doing – Having' model and notice the differences.

The keys to success in changing your limiting beliefs are:

- Be aware of those beliefs that limit you.
- Think about the ultimate cost of holding these limiting beliefs.
- Think about an alternative belief that you really can hold to be true.
- Practise thinking about the new belief whenever you can and relate to the benefits of holding it.

It might surprise you how quickly the new belief becomes a habit!

brilliant recap

Your beliefs and values are at the centre of your performance. The key points covered in this chapter include:

- Our values are those things we feel are important.
- Money should be in the value set of a successful salesperson.
- Beliefs are those things we feel are true. They are formed around our values and are often not objectively true – they are just true for us.
- Beliefs can support or limit our performance.
- We can change those beliefs that limit us.
- The first step in changing limiting beliefs is to be aware of them and to realise the ultimate cost of holding them.
- Look for objective evidence to the contrary of the limiting belief – examples of when it has not been true, the exceptions.
- Think about alternative beliefs that we can hold to be true and be aware of these when we are selling.

CHAPTER 3

Performance and selling

Imagine this scenario for a moment. You have just finished a lengthy sales meeting with your boss. You have been left in no doubt that you have to hit the quarterly revenue target. He is under pressure and, therefore, so are you. In fact, you spent most of the meeting discussing the revenue number and the prospects and whether one prospect was 80% likely to close this quarter or 70% likely. The discussion was about the ranking and the likelihood of the deal closing. Sound familiar? This is a meeting about 'results'.

It is often said that 'sales is all about results'. In a very real way this is true, of course. The only problem is, we cannot 'do' a result. If the sole focus of our attention is the number, the target, or sector penetration percentage then we might know when we have got there (because it is likely to be measurable) but achieving the objective is dependent upon our performance – those things that we do that either contribute or detract from our achieving the result.

Contrast this with a meeting that outlines the result (you need to hit the number) and then discusses your specific action plan for each account. Maybe for one the focus is on the next meeting and how you can plan and prepare. Maybe for another it is brainstorming how you can reach the decision maker and what might influence them the most. This latter scenario is focusing on different aspects of performance that will then help maximise the chance of achieving the result or objective that you want.

'A bad manager confuses activity with performance.' – Anon

What makes a focus on performance so effective is that **you are in control of it**. Think about an Olympic swimmer training for the 400m freestyle event. Clearly the result he / she will want is to win the event. But the swimmer cannot control that outcome because there are seven other swimmers in the same pool. The swimmer must set a performance goal of which he / she is in control that, if achieved, makes the result they want most likely to happen.

keep focused on only those things that you can control or influence

A number of things contribute to performance in sales and you need to keep focused on only those things that you can control or influence. For most people, the following diagram helps illustrate what these components of performance are.

The performance iceberg

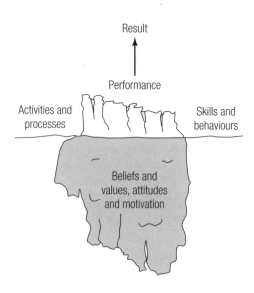

Result

Performance

Activities and processes

Skills and behaviours

Beliefs and values, attitudes and motivation

The visible things that contribute to our sales performance (i.e. those things that are above the surface and can be observed) are the processes and activities we follow and the skills and behaviours we demonstrate and use.

Processes and activities

Selling requires a process to sit behind it. Without a process we cannot manage the different aspects of the sale and, therefore, our performance in each aspect. We may have preferences for certain parts of the sales process, and monitoring our activities and the process steps we follow is a quick way to start improving our performance immediately.

We cover the sales process in detail in Part 2 but some specific aspects of performance on which we can focus, in terms of process and activities, include:

- Do we pay equal attention to each stage of the sales process or focus on one to the exclusion of others?
- Do we make enough calls to new prospects to get the meetings we require?
- Do we always follow-up after sending a quote?
- Do we ensure that we update the records after each call?

Skills and behaviours

In carrying out sales process steps and activities we use a variety of observable behaviours and skills to help achieve a result. A number of these are covered in Part 3 but they include:

- The extent to which we build rapport (a harmonious connection) with the other person.
- Our ability to use effective questioning to uncover buyer needs.
- Our ability to influence the buyer to see the benefits of the product or service we are selling.

- Our effectiveness on the telephone to secure a meeting.
- The way in which we conduct our meetings, including how much we speak relative to the prospect.

Like all good icebergs, only the tip is visible and a great deal more exists beneath the surface. We cannot see these things directly but we can definitely see the impact of them.

Beliefs and values

An awareness of our beliefs and values helps us understand certain patterns of behaviours and results that we achieve. For example, if we believe that we cannot cold call, it is likely that we will avoid that activity. No amount of skills or process will help!

Attitude

This is another very important but often unseen contributor to sales performance. What is our attitude to dealing with clients? What about our attitude to work generally? When a customer requests more information and perhaps does this more than once, what is our attitude towards them? We are in control of our attitude and it is something of which we need to be aware.

We are in control of our attitude

Motivation

What gets you up in the morning? It is our motivation that provides the energy for our work and it is often linked with our values. For example, sometimes, when I need a bit more motivation to go the extra mile, I think about the great family holiday that I am planning and for which I need the money!

If you are serious about improving your performance, you need to look at each of these areas objectively and take action where required.

↗ brilliant exercise

Use the template in the free resource pack (email **resources@brilliant-selling.com** to receive this pack) or create your own to list objectively the following:

1   What are the key results on which I am judged (sales revenues, margin, new clients, etc.)?

2   Process / activities: being objective, what are the process steps or activities in my selling that I do not focus on enough?

3   Skills / behaviours: reflect on the last two weeks and think about the skills and behaviours you use in your daily sales work. Use the list below as a start point and add your own skills / behaviours to it.

- Building rapport.

- Questioning skills.

- Listening skills.

- Talking about benefits rather than features.

- Taking time to uncover needs before trying to present products.

Prioritise the list in terms of where your efforts on developing the skill/behaviour will have most impact. Write down specific actions for the top three and remind yourself to do these (put in your diary a reminder to focus on preparing three great questions before each meeting every day, for a week, for example). Better still; seek objective feedback from a colleague or manager on what your priorities should be.

Print this out and add to it – make it a regular source of your personal reflection and it will pay dividends.

A final warning about a focus exclusively on results is illustrated with this story. Years ago, I was selling consumer products to retail outlets. I had been having a good year but was slightly behind on the current quarter. If I could hit that quarter I would get a bonus and my sales manager kept reminding me of it and encouraging me to push for every sale I could. I went in to one customer where I had developed a good relationship and, with my sales manager's results focused words in my mind, I managed to sell a significant amount of product for them to stock. I was happy. I had hit my quarterly number and made my bonus. Unfortunately, the customer could not sell the product and it was the last time they bought from me. I had sacrificed the relationship and future sales for that one result.

One thing we have not discussed here but which is very relevant to performance is the setting of specific and appropriate goals. We cover this in detail in Part 2 on planning. We would encourage you to apply the principles detailed there to your own personal performance in terms of behaviours, skills, activities and processes. More information on this can be found on the **www.brilliant-selling.com** website and by using the templates contained in the free resource pack (which you can receive by sending an email to **resources@brilliant-selling.com**).

Awareness and responsibility – the keys for continual improvement

Everything we have talked about in this chapter requires you to put your attention on those aspects of what you do – your performance – that contribute to achieving a result. This brings us to a key point about improving performance. There are two things that you must have to bring about any change in behaviour (or belief): **awareness** and **responsibility**.

The performance iceberg gives labels to different aspects of performance but it all comes down to these two words.

Awareness

I can only change a behaviour or belief if I am first aware of what I am doing. Sounds obvious but we all do things of which we are not consciously aware. If we are not aware of them we cannot change them. Take an example of someone who seems consistently to get to the stage of making a proposal but not winning the business. They think they are doing everything right until one helpful prospect gives them feedback on why they lost the deal: 'The other suppliers asked questions that uncovered our real business needs. You had a good product but we did not feel you fully understood our challenges.' Some salespeople would simply listen to the feedback, put it down to experience and go on to the next opportunity, choosing not to learn from the experience. A Brilliant Salesperson would ask more questions and raise his awareness on an aspect of his performance that is limiting his result. The Brilliant Salesperson might choose to change his approach with the next prospect and, whatever the outcome, seek feedback on that aspect of his work – possibly by bringing a colleague in to observe.

The great news is that, as soon as you put your awareness on something, your performance on that aspect of your work automatically and unconsciously improves! Imagine that! Putting an aspect of your performance under the magnifying glass improves it almost without trying. Think back to learning how to drive a car. The first few times you try to pull away smoothly and find the right balance between letting out the clutch and depressing the accelerator may not have been as smooth as you would have liked. But, in a remarkably short period of time (hopefully), by putting your attention on it you simply improve naturally and easily.

Responsibility

This can be written another way: response-ability. In order to take responsibility for your own performance you need to realise that you have a response-ability, a choice of how you act and respond in any given situation. Remember, we work largely from unconscious habits and so we need to think about our actions if we are to see that there are other ways of responding. If, as has been my habit in the past, I consistently created quotations with lots of detail but without summarising the key and compelling reasons why the customer should buy from me, I do have a choice to change it if I want. I might ignore regular feedback from colleagues justifying my action in any number of ways but I do have a choice.

brilliant tips

- Seek objective feedback from your prospects, clients and colleagues. Challenge them to be specific about what they observe and what you could do differently.

- Really practise noticing the impact of everything you do – especially the conversations you have with clients and prospects.

- When you do not get the result that you want, think about what other choices you have so that you can respond differently next time.

We elaborate on this in the next chapter – self-coaching.

brilliant recap

The key points covered in this chapter concerning performance are:

- A focus on performance and not just result will bring about the improvements you want.
- Performance is made up of visible activities, processes, skills and behaviours as well as often invisible beliefs, attitudes and motivations.
- Your beliefs, attitudes and motivations have a bigger impact on your performance than the visible components.
- The two keys to improving performance are responsibility (response-ability) and awareness.
- Putting your awareness on something automatically improves your performance.

CHAPTER 4

Continually improve through self-coaching

B rilliant Salespeople engage in self-coaching all of the time – even if they do not call it that.

Coaching has emerged in recent years as a popular development tool. Whilst it came from the world of sport, its application and success in business relates to its focus on increasing responsibility and awareness. Whilst lots of businesses employ coaches to help senior managers it is also something that you can use very effectively on yourself.

Some of you will have a sales manager and others will not. Even if you do report to a sales manager the chances are that you are, to a large extent, left to your own devices. You need to achieve the sales result with limited input and support from your colleagues. The previous chapter talked about the importance of awareness and responsibility in improving performance and, therefore, the result you achieve. For most, this improvement in performance is largely going to be down to you. So, learn how to self-coach.

'Five frogs are sitting on a log. Four decide to jump off. How many are left? Answer: five. Why? Because there's a difference between deciding and doing.' – Mark L. Feldman and Michael F. Spratt, *Five Frogs on a Log*

The intention with your self-coaching is to raise awareness and response-ability through reflecting on what it is that you do.

> raise awareness and response-ability through reflecting on what it is that you do

There are primarily two uses of self-coaching that the Brilliant Salesperson focuses on: general development leading to continuous improvement, and specific development of a skill or ability.

General development leading to continuous improvement

This involves creating the habit of reflecting – often at the end of each day or after a sales call or other meeting. The intention is to become much more aware of, objectively, how you perform. This requires you asking questions and taking the time fully to consider the answers, noticing and challenging any assumptions.

Two examples of how you can use this to improve are:

After a sales meeting with a prospect
Take a few minutes immediately after you finish the meeting (resist the urge to put it off until later – do this while the meeting is still fresh in your mind) to ask yourself some key questions on different aspects of the meeting, so that you can become more, objectively, aware of how you performed. These questions might include:

- Did I meet my objective for the call? If not, what specifically could I have done in hindsight to have improved my chances?
- Considering my planning of the meeting, to what extent was my goal for the meeting appropriate and realistic? What could I have done in my planning to have improved the outcome?
- What did I do well in the meeting?

- What have I learned from the meeting about my approach, skills and behaviours?
- What did I do, specifically, that moved the relationship forward?

At the end of each day

Take five minutes at the end of every day to reflect on the day and your performance. Developing this habit is probably the quickest way to improve your abilities and success. Questions that you can ask here include:

- What did I do really well today?
- What is one thing that I have learned from today?
- What will I do differently in future as a result of today?

Specific development of a skill or ability

When you have identified a particular skill or activity around which you want to improve, then you can focus your self-coaching on this. The process is the same as for general development but with the addition of some specific goals, that you set for yourself in advance, around the skill or activity.

An example of this might be your ability to establish the right first impression.

First of all, you need to define what the 'right' first impression is that you want to create. It may be that this relates to establishing credibility early on with the prospect. This may require you to know something about their business and that you show this in the first five minutes of the conversation with them. You might then want to consider how well you think you are doing at this right now. On a scale of 1–10 where 10 is 'totally credible', where do you think you are now? Where do you want to be on this 'credibility with my prospects' scale in, say, two months?

Once you have a specific goal you can then hold the meeting and reflect on how well you did. Questions you might ask yourself after the meeting in this example include:

- What did I do to establish credibility in the meeting and when did I do this?
- What was the impact of this that I observed in the prospect (what did I see and hear)?
- Did the behaviour achieve the objective as far as I can tell? If not, what could I do more of / less of / differently next time?

> Making self-coaching a personal habit will dramatically improve your performance

Making self-coaching a personal habit will dramatically improve your performance – all for an investment of five minutes a day! Why would you not do this?

Feedback from colleagues

If self-coaching is something that you can choose to do every day, without needing the support of anyone, then seeking opportunities to get feedback from your colleagues or sales manager is something you should do whenever you get the opportunity.

It is surprising how little feedback we get that we can use to our benefit. Often this is because the person giving the feedback has not been trained on how to give effective feedback. Great feedback is both objective and specific. Feedback such as 'you did really well in that meeting' is next to useless. Feedback such as 'you really engaged the prospect around how we could help him' is better but still lacks the specifics that make it really useful. Feedback such as 'when you asked questions about their business and then linked our product to solving his biggest problem' is much better because it tells you specifically what you did that was good. This is the same for feedback on those things you want to improve. A colleague giving feedback such as 'At the start of the meeting I noticed that you asked two questions [gives you examples] and when the prospect didn't answer immediately you gave him two alternative answers,' is much more useful than 'You need to work on your questioning skills'.

The point here is that it is up to *you* to ask for the feedback you want from your colleagues or manager. Do not assume that a) they will give it to you at all and b) they know how to give you great feedback.

If you get an opportunity to be accompanied during your sales activities at any time, then decide the specific areas on which you would value feedback. Ensure that you get specific, observable, objective feedback. This kind of feedback is a real gift. Truly objective feedback from someone other than yourself can make a real difference to your awareness and performance.

'You cannot teach a man anything. You can only help him discover it within himself.' – Galileo

🡕 brilliant recap

Self-coaching is guaranteed to improve your sales performance. In this section, we have discovered:

- Brilliant salespeople self-coach and it takes only five minutes a day.

- Self-coaching raises your awareness through you asking good open questions about your own performance and reflecting objectively on the answers.

- You can use it for general development (by reviewing your day) or to develop specific skills.

- Seeking feedback from colleagues is another way to help coach yourself.

- Be explicit about what feedback you want and ensure it is both objective and specific.

PART 2

Process and planning

attended a meeting with a prospect some years ago. I arrived at her office with very little time to spare (because I had not planned my journey or the time it would take) and spent a few rushed minutes in the car preparing an agenda (which I should have sent in advance). When I did meet the prospect, I had not planned any of my questions and so failed to drive the meeting in the way that I needed. I did not get the business!

I also remember managing a sales team in which I had two very different individuals. One spoke to lots of prospects, submitted lots of proposals and won a good deal of business. He succeeded through working very hard and having so many prospects that in any given month a number would buy from him. But, he never really knew who it would be. He was spinning a number of plates and putting his attention on the ones most likely to fall rather than planning a systematic approach to achieve the result he wanted. The other had fewer prospects but would know very specifically where they were in the sales process and what her next step was. Her accuracy was impressive and she always seemed to make her long-term forecast. When you are managing a business, predictability is absolutely critical and I came to value her accuracy very highly. Over time, because she had knowledge of her prospects and where they were in the sales process, we could work to improve her results.

The first story is about planning and the second is about process. When we were researching this book we were looking for some inspirational quotes for each section and it became apparent that there were not many inspirational quotes concerning process and planning! It is fair to say that a lot of sales people do not enjoy or see the value of a focus on process and planning. Whilst the words 'process' and 'planning' might not be synonymous with inspiration, they are critical within the context of Brilliant Selling. Process and planning done well:

- Underpin and provide structure to all of the activities that you carry out towards achieving your desired result.
- Help keep the real priorities in the front of your mind.
- Ensure that you get the best possible result from the activities in which you engage.

This section will answer questions including:

- What are the key stages of the sales process, why are they important and what are my priorities in each?
- How do I make the most effective use of my time?
- What aspects of my work will really benefit from time spent on planning?
- What sales-related information should I pay attention to and how can it help me achieve the results that I want?

A focus on process and planning takes relatively little time but it is often the difference between consistency in your selling and the stressful cycle of 'feast or famine' in sales results that some people experience. It is a big differentiator in Brilliant Salespeople.

CHAPTER 5

The sales process as a tool for improvement

W e all do things every day that involve process, including cleaning our teeth and getting ready for work. Some of these processes we do well and some not so well.

Whatever you sell, it is likely that there will be a series of steps that you can, or do, follow that take you from an initial conversation with a prospect through to the closing of a sale. There may be some specific nuances and process steps depending on the nature of your market, product, service and purchaser. In this section, we share with you a simple sales process that can be applied in a wide variety of sales environments. We encourage you to use it as a tool to raise your awareness as to where you can better spend your time to develop the results that you want, knowing that there may be some adaptation required on your part.

What's the point?

This is something that I have heard from salespeople in the past. They say things such as 'You can't put what I do into a simple process' and 'Every sale is different'. These comments may be true to some extent, but the main benefit of having and following a sales process is that we can monitor and measure our performance in each step. This enables us to focus on developing better results at each stage of the process, thereby improving our sales and our consistency.

'Success is a process more than a realisation.' – Anon

This diagram summarises the seven steps of the 'generic' sales process. Through all of the steps runs the thread of establishing and building rapport and credibility. The fact is that you need to demonstrate these at every step of the sales process. We discuss rapport and credibility in Part 3 of this book.

We look at each step of the process and provide a summary of what the step involves, what some of the common problems or issues experienced in that step are and what your key priorities should be.

1 Prospecting

Prospect

↓

Identify needs and implications

↓

Present solutions

↓

Meet objections

↓

Negotiate

↓

Ask for the business

↓

Manage the account

Whilst different definitions of prospecting exist, our view is that the term encompasses all of the activities related to defining, targeting and developing prospects for your product or service. For most salespeople, if you do not spend enough time prospecting you can easily run out of customers. Even when times are good we need to fill the funnel with new prospects so that customers continue to buy from us.

What does it involve?

1 **Identifying possible prospects**: before you can attract prospects, you need to identify a prospect profile. There will be a number of questions depending on your situation and market but they are likely to include variations of the following:

- Who, specifically, will buy from me?
- Why, specifically, will they buy from me?
- Where, specifically, will I find them?
- How, specifically, will I know them from other people who are less likely to buy from me?

Do you notice a theme in the questions? That word 'specifically' is critical to answer. The tighter we can define our prospects the more focused and successful our sales efforts are likely to be.

2 **Targeting possible prospects**: having identified possible prospects we need to effectively target them. What is the best way for them to receive a compelling message about what we are offering that enables us to start a dialogue?

3 **Developing prospects**: we need to qualify them in or out of our sales process. We need to make a decision on how likely they are to buy from us. Above all, we need to be objective at this point. It is easy to fool ourselves into thinking that everyone we talk to is a possible sale but if we do not qualify objectively we waste time that could be spent with people who are more likely to buy! We need to establish qualification criteria – aspects that we know to be true or untrue for most people who would buy from us.

What are some common problems?

- **Not being really clear on the prospect profile**: we waste time talking to people who may be unlikely to buy.
- **Being clear about our prospect profile but not acting on it**: we can engage in activities with people that we know are unlikely to buy from us.
- **Not doing enough activity**: when sales are good we might 'ease off' on prospecting activity. This leads to a 'feast or famine' result.

- **Not qualifying early enough**: if we do not qualify our prospects objectively we will have too many people going through the other stages of the sales process and

> Make sure you engage in enough prospecting activity

will not be able to manage them all effectively. It is far better to put fewer prospects through into the sales pipeline but know they are the right ones to spend your time on!

What are your key priorities?

- **Make sure you engage in enough prospecting activity**: you must make time for prospecting if you are to achieve consistent sales results. It is not simply something to do when the sales are not coming in.
- **Be objective in your qualification of prospects**: be realistic and make decisions on objective criteria.

Outcome

The outcome from this first stage of the sales process is qualified prospects that enter the sales pipeline to be managed through the other steps of the sales process.

Part 4 of this book is focused on prospecting and will give you more detail on this important aspect of Brilliant Selling.

2 Identifying needs and implications

This step in the process is about discovery. The key skills that you use will be questioning and listening. Before somebody makes a decision to buy something they need a good reason. The product or service will either do something that they want or it will prevent something that they do not want. In either case, the reasons for taking the action you want them to take must outweigh the reasons for inaction. They need to see the **value** in what you are offering.

You need to take the time fully to understand their needs and, through further questioning, help them see the implications of these needs, if they are not met.

What does it involve?

1 **Discovery**: finding out more about the prospect and their specific needs through questioning and listening skills.

2 **Building the motivation to make a buying decision**: asking more questions will help turn a need into something that motivates the person to take action; to want to buy. They need to see the benefits of taking action.

What are some common problems?

● **We do not ask enough questions**: we move too quickly into discussing our product or service and we cannot link it effectively with their needs or give them a big enough reason to take action.

● **We make assumptions**: we think we know what they need and what is important to them so we either do not ask or we

ask closed questions, which reduce our rapport and
credibility with them.

What are your key priorities?

- **To understand fully their needs**: this will enable you to
  personalise how you present the solution to them in the next
  stage of the process.
- **To have helped them build a compelling reason to take
  action**: they must be motivated to act **before** we position
  our product or service to them.

Outcome

A motivated prospect who understands why they need to
take action.

Part 3 of this book looks in more detail at the skills of questioning, listening and needs analysis.

3 Present solutions

Prospect
↓
Identify needs and implications
↓
Present solutions
↓
Meet objections
↓
Negotiate
↓
Ask for the business
↓
Manage the account

Presenting your solution involves building a compelling case which confirms why **your** solution is the ideal fit for the prospect and their needs. Important at this stage is to consider things from the prospect's perspective rather than your own. This stage may be part of the same discussion as the needs identification or it might be a separate meeting or discussion. The key skills here are influencing, and you can only influence effectively if you have all of the facts from the prospect to form the basis for your presentation.

What does it involve?

1 **Articulating benefits**: being clear on how your product or service answers the prospect's needs specifically.

2 **Gauging their reaction objectively**: so that you can assess their interest and on what you need to focus.

3 **Providing a written proposal**: in some cases this might be necessary and could be either a formal proposal or something much more succinct.

4 **Presenting**: you may need to present to an individual or a group.

What are some common problems?

- **We make assumptions**: assumptions might include that the prospect knows why our product or service is the best, that we know what is important to them and that we know how they buy this type of product or service.

- **We communicate features**: we present what the product or solution does rather than how it benefits the prospect.

- **We do not present to the right person(s)**: we do not take account of other decision makers or possible steps in the buying process.

What are your key priorities?

- **Articulate the benefits in the prospect's terms**: use their words from the discovering needs phase to link your product or service to their requirements.

- **Uncover** any additional steps or information needed to progress the sale.

> Articulate the benefits in the prospect's terms: use their words

- **Influence the decision maker**: so that the value or benefit of your product or service outweighs the 'cost' of doing nothing (this might be in emotional or hard business terms).

Outcome

To convince the buyer of the benefits of your product or service and identify what you need to do in order to close the sale.

Presenting solutions is covered in more detail in Part 5 of this book.

4 Meet objections

Prospect
↓
Identify needs and implications
↓
Present solutions
↓
Meet objections
↓
Negotiate
↓
Ask for the business
↓
Manage the account

A lot of sales training courses talk about 'overcoming' or 'busting' objections but this implies they are barriers rather than enablers to your sale. An objection is often simply a request for more information. Objections are a natural part of the sales process and they show the prospect is interested and considering how they could take your product or service forward.

What does it involve?

1 **Surface and welcome objections**: if you do not surface objections you cannot handle them effectively.

2 **Fully understand them**: you will need to ask more questions to understand the objection clearly.

3 **Address them correctly and fully**: you need to take them seriously and make sure you answer them.

4 **Check with the prospect**: do not move on until you know the prospect is satisfied that the objection has been addressed.

What are some common problems?

● **We avoid objections**: we might fear them and so try to avoid dealing with them.

● **We do not deal with them effectively**: we give an answer but do not check that it has truly addressed the prospect's concerns.

What are your key priorities?

● **To welcome them**: how you feel about objections will impact on how you handle them. Think of them as requests for more information.

● **To take the time to address them**: address them fully and not with a cursory answer that you think might do the job.

- **Not to move on before you know they have been addressed**: unless you address the objections the prospect will still have doubt in their mind – moving on too quickly will reduce your chance of making the sale.

Outcome

To leave the prospect with no substantive reason not to buy. To enable you to start the negotiation / asking for the business stages with no outstanding issues (other than terms).

Part 5 of this book covers objections in more detail.

5 Negotiate

Prospect
↓
Identify needs and implications
↓
Present solutions
↓
Meet objections
↓
Negotiate
↓
Ask for the business
↓
Manage the account

Technically, negotiation is not something you aim to do as part of the sales process. This might sound strange but the ideal is to have the prospect emotionally bought into your product or service before you start negotiating. If they have agreed, in principle, to buying, then the negotiation is about the terms. If you negotiate too early, it can link the purchase **decision** to the terms; making it likely that you will need to discount or make other concessions.

What does it involve?

1 **Reaching agreement on the terms**: terms can encompass many things other than price; negotiation relates to gaining agreement on the total package (whatever that might be).

2 **Trading concessions**: to agree terms you may need to give something to the prospect (an increase in payment terms, for example). In return for this you would ask the client for something (to commit to purchasing a certain quantity, for example).

What are some common problems?

- **We assume we will need to negotiate**: this leads us to talking discounts before they are requested. Salespeople can be far too accommodating!

- **Thinking it is *all* about price**: do not deduce their intentions from your fears – buying is often not about price but emotion.

- **Not linking the product to the value it brings for the prospect**: we constantly need to make this link and not get into discussing terms in isolation of what the purchase will bring the customer.

- **Giving rather than trading**: we can give in to requests for discounts or better payment terms without asking for something in return. This can set a precedent in the relationship.

What are your key priorities?

- **To reach an agreement that works well for both parties**: not one that just works for you **or** the prospect.

Outcome

To clear the way to securing the sale.

Negotiation is covered in more detail in Part 3 of this book.

6 Closing and gaining commitment

Prospect
↓
Identify needs and implications
↓
Present solutions
↓
Meet objections
↓
Negotiate
↓
Ask for the business
↓
Manage the account

If you do the other stages of the sales process well, with rapport and credibility throughout, this is the easy part. The main point here is actually to ask for the sale.

What does it involve?

1 **Check that you have met all of the objections**: before you ask for the order it makes sense to check that all of their questions have been addressed to their satisfaction.

2 **Choose how best to ask for the sale**: think about what would work most effectively.

3 **Ask!**

What are some common problems?

- **We might put off asking**: we may not feel comfortable asking for the sale and this might lead us either to put off asking for the sale or make our request sound more like an apology.

- **We might ask too early**: if we ask before we have met all objections we might get a 'no'.

What are your key priorities?

- To consider when to ask and how to ask.
- To gain commitment!

Outcome

To secure a sale in which all parties win.

Gaining commitment is covered in more detail in Part 5 of this book.

7 Manage the account

Prospect

↓

Identify needs and implications

↓

Present solutions

↓

Meet objections

↓

Negotiate

↓

Ask for the business

↓

Manage the account

For some of you each sale will be to a new customer but, for a lot of people, selling is about creating a relationship that might lead to more than one sale. If this is the case for you, then managing the customer relationship is an important stage of the sales process. It is five times easier to sell to an existing customer than to win new ones and so that means it is well worth the effort.

What does it involve?

1 **Focus on the relationship**: if a customer feels you are only interested in selling to her she is unlikely to see value in the relationship and may well go elsewhere in future. Stay in touch as regularly as is appropriate. Make sure you know the right people in the customer's business and form relationships to help develop your position.

2 **Look to add value**: how you do this will differ depending on your market but successful account managers look to add value to their customers every time they can.

What are some common problems?

- **Not making time for it**: this is an important task but never urgent so we often focus on other things.

- **Focusing on only one person**: we leave ourselves exposed if we only focus on one person. What if they leave? Where is our relationship then?

What are your key priorities?

- **Develop the relationship to greater levels of trust**: we need to set goals around developing the relationship so that we erect barriers for the competition and maximise the chances of future business.

Outcome

This might differ depending on your particular situation but we are looking for a broad and deep customer relationship built on trust, which will yield additional sales.

Managing the customer is covered in more detail in Part 6 of this book.

brilliant recap

Having and following a simple sales process is good for our results. Whilst the specific process that you follow might have some differences from the process we have covered here, the key points are:

- Having well-defined steps in a sales process enables you to monitor and measure your performance in each step more objectively, thereby improving your performance and consistency.
- Rapport and credibility are needed by Brilliant Salespeople at every step of the sales process.
- Our ability to make assumptions is a common problem for salespeople at each step of the process – we are seeking objectivity to improve performance.

CHAPTER 6

Making the most of your time

One thing that we often hear from salespeople is that there is never enough time to do everything. In sales, there are always more things that we can do: more prospects to call, more customers we could visit, more administration that could complete. One of the big issues that Brilliant Salespeople have mastered is how to make the very best use of their time. They know where to spend time for the greatest return and they do not confuse activity with results.

> they do not confuse activity with results

Time is one of those things that is finite. We cannot change it. The very best that we can do is to understand where we spend our time now and consider if it is on the right things. Our habits, combined with external and internal pressures, lead us to spending time on some activities at the expense of other activities. Having made some decisions on what the 'right things' are, we can then choose to change our habits to ensure that the right things get done.

'Time is money.' – Benjamin Franklin

What can you control?

In his book *The 7 Habits of Highly Effective People* Stephen Covey details what it is that effective people seem to do habitually. One of these habits is that effective people focus their time only on those things that they can control or influence. If you think about it, this is common sense but how often have you found yourself fretting or spending time worrying about things that you can do nothing about? The Brilliant Salesperson recognises when they are doing this and they stop. He or she focuses on an aspect of the situation over which they have some influence. For example, in an economic downturn, it is easy to focus a lot of time worrying about how bad things are and how competitors are hungry for the business that you are also chasing. If you ask yourself what you can control about the situation, you might realise that the economy is the same for everyone and that your efforts are best placed deepening prospect and existing customer relationships. This activity might develop more of a competitive edge for you. Whilst this approach will not make the problem go away, it does put you in a stronger situation because you are choosing to focus on something you can action.

> spend your time on those things that you can impact and change

brilliant tip

For any problem that you find yourself facing, ask yourself 'Over what aspect of this problem or issue do I have some control or influence?' and focus your time on that aspect. If you have no control, then move on and spend your time on those things that you can impact and change.

What are the 'right' things?

Once we have made a commitment to focus only on things we can control, we can turn our attention to the choices we are making. Where do we spend our time now? Often, we spend time on those things we are good at or enjoy. We also spend time on things that we are pressured to do by others. Over time it is easy to become reactive and not make conscious choices over the things to which we focus time and attention.

With limited time and a need to maximise our effectiveness and performance we need to make conscious choices. But how? And if we are not doing the right things now, how will we make the time for them? It is not as if we have lots of spare time to fill!

> it is not the activity that counts, it is the result you achieve

We have to start by questioning our prioritisation. In addition to making choices based on what we prefer to do, we are likely to be responding to things we perceive as being urgent. But these are not necessarily going to move our sales forward. Things that move sales forward are important and not necessarily urgent. Some examples of important, but not urgent, things include:

- Reflecting on our performance at the end of each day to define what worked well and what we will do differently tomorrow.
- Planning an agenda for a prospect meeting.
- Researching a prospect's company so that we know more about his or her business.
- Setting specific goals around a stage in the sales process where we know we need to improve.

In a busy day it is easy to see how such things get missed. Brilliant Salespeople make sure these important but not urgent tasks get done. Remember, it is not the activity that counts, it is the result you achieve from your activity.

'People can generally make time for what they choose to do; it is not really the time but the will that is lacking.' – Sir John Lubbock

Make time for the right things

The next logical question, once we have identified the things on which we should focus to maximise our result, is how we make the time to do these things. The secret is not to try and release huge chunks of time because this is simply not realistic. Perhaps the most that we can expect (from re-prioritising the things we focus on at present) is to find another 15–20 minutes per day to spend on the important tasks. If this is going to work, we need to make sure that the goals we set around these tasks are manageable; remembering that anything we do is likely to bring a benefit.

Table 6.1 sets out some examples of what these goals might be.

Important task	Possible 20-minute goals
Increase the number of prospects contacted that agree to meet with me	– Monitor my call results so that I have accurate data on my ratio of prospects to meetings (5 minutes) – Ask my manager to listen to my calls and give objective feedback (15 minutes) – Reflect on my calls immediately after making them to identify what worked and what did not work (5 minutes)
Increase the number of prospects that I can visit in a day	– Create a specific agenda for my meeting so I stay focused and manage the meeting time (10 minutes) – Plan trips further in advance so that I can obtain more prospects to visit in the area (ongoing but no more than 5 minutes a day)
Improve my conversion ratio	– Review the last 6 months' prospect and sales order numbers so that I know my conversion ratio and set a target ratio based on this (15 minutes) – Focus on coming up with some great open questions to use in needs identification (15 minutes) – Consider the regular objections I get and amend how I present the product to manage these better (20 minutes x 3 days)

Table 6.1 Possible 20-minute goals around major tasks

It is easy to come up with the short-term goals that will make the difference and you then simply need to put these tasks in your diary and commit to taking action. You will find that the more you choose to set these manageable goals around important tasks, the more likely you are to achieve them. Over time, this will make a dramatic, positive difference to your performance and result.

brilliant exercise

Make a list of the important but non-urgent tasks that would make a real difference to your performance. Get as specific as you can in terms of what you need to do. Break the task down into smaller, short-term goals that you ▶

could accomplish in 20 minutes. Prioritise them based on their likely positive impact and put them in your diary. Commit to doing at least one of them this week.

'Things which matter most should never be at the mercy of things which matter least.' – J.F. Goethe

---

⊿ brilliant recap

How we manage and use our time has a direct and significant impact on our sales performance and results. In this section we have covered the following points:

- Brilliant salespeople spend time on the right things – they are proactive.

- Make a conscious effort to spend time focusing only on those things over which you have some control or influence. Spending time focusing or worrying about things you cannot control is wasteful and detracts from your results.

- Consider how you prioritise and on what activities you spend your time now. Often this is on things we either enjoy doing or are under pressure to deliver. This is not the same as focusing on important tasks that move your business forward.

- To spend more time on the important, non-urgent tasks, you need first to define what they are.

- Break these important tasks into small goals that will take no more than 20 minutes a day to action.

- Over a period of time, the '20 minutes a day' actions will add up to making a significant positive impact on your sales performance.

CHAPTER 7

Planning for success

Planning implies coming up with a method, procedure or approach in advance of taking action. Perhaps a good example of the benefits of planning is this quote from the entrepreneur Donald Trump:

'When I started out in business, I spent a great deal of time researching every detail that might be pertinent to the deal I was interested in making. I still do the same today. People often comment on how quickly I operate, but the reason I can move quickly is that I've done the background work first, which no one usually sees. I prepare myself thoroughly, and then when it is time to move ahead, I am ready to sprint.'

Planning is another one of those things we know that we should do and convince ourselves we are doing well enough. The Brilliant Salesperson plans for actions rather than results and he makes plans around the important things. In sales, a lot of 'plans' are actually targets. We might have a sales plan that relates to a revenue or margin figure, for example. We need to plan the aspects of our sales work so that we can achieve the results that we want. Almost every aspect of what we do could benefit from a plan. The major benefit of planning is that we can be more objective and thoughtful about what we need to do to achieve our goals and ensure that we do not miss out important aspects that could make a difference.

> Almost every aspect of what we do could benefit from a plan

'Planning is bringing the future into the present so that you can do something about it now.' – Alan Lakein

Let us look at some specific things we can plan and what we should take account of when we are planning. These are examples rather than a definitive list.

Planning prospecting activities

We can plan a number of aspects of our prospecting activity, as suggested in the table.

The time needed to prospect	By taking the sales target and dividing it by the average order value you can arrive at the number of sales you need to make. By using current conversion rates, you can come up with a total number of prospects that you need to contact. You can then factor the time taken to generate a prospect (maybe through your own prospecting activity such as cold calling) to arrive at the amount of time required. This activity can then be planned into your calendar.
	So, if my average order value is £1,000 and I have a new account sales target for the year of £200,000, then I know I need 200 sales over 12 months to achieve target. If I know that for every 3 prospects I have, I convert 1 into a sale, then I need 200 x 3 prospects to make my sales target. Now I can plan how much time it will take to generate 600 prospects using current or potential prospecting activities.
Our strategy for contact	We might plan how we should best make contact with our prospects. We may have an existing strategy but choose to brainstorm new ideas to get to the same or a different type of purchaser. Based on the outcome of this brainstorming we can then come up with a detailed plan.
Our key messages	We can plan how best to communicate the benefits and differentiators of our product or service to potential customers. Different types of customer might be interested in different messages.

How to improve conversion rates	Once we know our conversion rates we can make a plan that can help improve them. This might include changing aspects of our sales process and reviewing results, for example.

Table 7.1 Some aspects of prospecting activity

Planning meetings

Brilliant Salespeople make time to plan their meetings so that they maximise the chance of achieving their objectives from them. This planning often does not take a lot of time but can make a significant difference. We know of lots of salespeople who do not plan in this area – they turn up and 'wing it'. For that small investment in planning they could dramatically improve their outcome.

Prospect meetings	Research the prospect, e.g. using the internet Set an agenda for the meeting Plan your key questions Think about who should be there Plan your own outcomes – what do you want to achieve?
Presenting solutions	Think about what the prospect needs to know Put yourself in the prospect's shoes to bring greater empathy Plan how you will make your points clear and compelling What questions might come up and how will you address them? If presenting with others, who will do what and how will you manage handovers?
Internal sales meetings	Do the necessary preparation Understand what is expected of you in the meeting Think about issues on the agenda so that you can contribute Look at, and action if appropriate, the minutes from the previous meeting

Table 7.2 Some types of meeting: kinds of preparation

Planning the efficient use of time

Client / prospect visits	Planning your territory and visits so that you maximise efficiency and use of your time
	Thinking about the time needed realistically to cover your meeting agenda
Customer contact	Planning how often you need to contact your clients and prospects and scheduling this activity
Administration	Taking things with you that you can do if you find yourself with a little time before or after a meeting or while you are travelling
	Planning time to do this aspect of your role

Table 7.3 Efficient use of time

 tip

Visit **www.brilliant-selling.com** for more ideas to inform your planning or use the templates within the free resource pack (send an email to **resources@brilliant-selling.com** to receive this pack).

Planning tips

'A good plan today is better than a perfect plan tomorrow.'

We are often planning in a changing environment. We are not likely to have perfect or complete information and we must resist the temptation to get into 'planning paralysis'. Do not let perfect be the enemy of the good. Often we create a plan only to find that it changes as soon as we start implementing it. This is fine. If we did not plan we would have a scattergun approach that would make it very difficult to review what is working and what we need to do differently. Once you have a plan that is good, it is best to implement it rather than try and improve it by another five percent from 85% to 90% perfect. Remember, you do not need to plan everything; you just need to plan the right things. Also,

> the best plans are often the simplest – they are easier to monitor

the best plans are often the simplest – they are easier to monitor. If you get into the habit of planning the important things, such as meeting agendas and thinking about the questions a prospect is likely to ask in a presentation, you will be surprised at how little time it adds and how much of a difference it makes!

'It pays to plan ahead. It wasn't raining when Noah built the ark.' – Anon.

Planning is best done in advance of the activity concerned. If you start to plan too late you are under pressure for a result and your planning will be far less effective. It is also difficult to be objective about a situation if you are planning in the middle of it.

⁊ brilliant recap

In this chapter on planning the key points that we covered were:

- A lot of plans are actually targets and what is missing is the thought about 'how' rather than 'what'.

- You should focus on making a good plan – do not get caught up with 'perfect'.

- Often the plans that make the most positive difference take the shortest time to compile. These include meeting agendas, possible questions a prospect might ask and researching the client so that you can add value.

- Planning in advance of an activity makes it easier to be more objective and to review the results afterwards.

CHAPTER 8

Setting the right goals

A while back I was in the market for a new car. I had gone through all the magazines and chosen the manufacturer, model, colour and specification. The next day I was travelling back from a sales call and it struck me how many of this specific colour, model and make of car I was seeing on the roads. The point is that these cars were on the road before I had made my choice. I was seeing these cars but my brain was simply not drawing them to my attention because I had not 'told it' they were of interest to me. Has this ever happened to you? After you set a goal and put your mind on something specific, your brain begins to notice those things that relate to the goal and your achievement of it. Bizarrely, my co-author Jeremy cannot visit any new town without automatically spotting hairdressing salons, as he used to work for L'Oréal!

Brilliant Salespeople set goals for themselves

'Without goals, and plans to reach them, you are like a ship that has set sail with no destination.' – Fitzhugh Dodson

Goal setting is critical in sales. We are often given sales goals in the form of targets but Brilliant Salespeople set goals for themselves. Goals come in many shapes and sizes and they can and should be set for any activity where you want to achieve a specific result. Goals focus our attention and tell our brain what is important to us so that it notices things that support its achievement.

Goals that get results

There are a few golden rules for setting brilliant goals and it is worth checking any goal that you set yourself against the following criteria.

● Is the goal in your control?
● Is the goal SMART?
● Does it motivate you?

Is the goal in your control?

Make sure that any goal is set around something of which you are in control. For example, if the outcome that you want is to be the top salesperson in your company or to be promoted to sales manager within a year, focus on the element of this outcome that you can control and set goals around it.

> goals we set have to be things we can control ourselves

Example	
Desired outcome	To be the top salesperson in the team.
What can I not control?	The sales figures of the other sales people.
What can I control?	My own performance relative to the amount of prospecting activity I do, the conversion rates I achieve and the average order value.
Possible goals	To spend a minimum of 3 hours each week between the hours of 8am and 9:30am on prospecting telephone calls To achieve a conversion rate from 'prospect' to 'qualified lead' of 3:1.
	To achieve an average order value of x or higher.

Aspirational outcomes are important – they give us inspiration and motivation but the goals we set have to be things we can control ourselves, that will take us toward the desired outcome.

Is the goal SMART?

SMART is an acronym for:

Specific: What do I want? In which situations? With which people? Make the goal as specific as you can. For example, 'I want to be successful' is not specific, whereas 'I want to achieve a client base of 40 customers in the local government sector with an average order value of x' is.

Measurable: How, specifically, will I know when I have achieved it? What are the measures?

Achievable: Is it a realistic goal for me to set? Can I achieve it? Do I need anybody's support or assistance?

Relevant: Is it relevant to my other goals, my aspirations, etc.?

Time bound: Pick a specific date rather than 'by the middle of next year'. The brain prefers a specific deadline.

Does it motivate you?

This might sound strange but not all goals motivate us. Sometimes we set a goal that is either so big or so far in the future that it does not seem 'real' enough to motivate us. It might be inspirational but sometimes we need to focus on goals where it is easier to see how we can achieve them. Make sure that you set milestone goals for those big, long-term goals you set. For example, if you want your product to be the market leader in a particular sector within a three-year timeframe, you might set milestones around the number and type of customer in the next 12 months, a minimum number of customer testimonials in year two, and so on. By setting smaller goals along the way to achieving the big one you can celebrate success, make sure you are on track and stay motivated.

What should we set goals for in our selling?

There are two main areas of our sales work where goals make real sense:

● Our individual performance.

● What we want from specific situations.

Individual performance

Break your sales performance down and set specific goals around the aspects that you most want to develop or that will make the biggest positive difference. These might include:

● The amount of time I spend in prospecting activity.

● The conversion rate I achieve at each stage of the sales process.

● My sales revenue achievement.

● The number and quality of open questions I ask to identify needs.

● The number of customers I talk to each week.

● The number of times that I ask for, and receive, referrals from existing customers.

● The number of board level contacts I make in each of my customers.

What we want from specific situations

Think about specific sales situations you approach, or are faced with, and set goals for them. These include:

● What I want to achieve from this sales meeting with my prospect.

- What I want to gain from visiting this networking event.
- What I want to find out from my research on this prospect.
- What I want to learn from attending this training course specifically.
- What I want to get done by the end of today.

brilliant tip

Visit **www.brilliant-selling.com** for more ideas on goal setting and use the templates in the free resource pack (send an email to **resources@brilliant-selling.com** to receive this pack).

'Think little goals and expect little achievements. Think big goals and win big success. – Abraham Lincoln

Brilliant Salespeople make goal setting a habit: each year, each month, each week, each day and each meeting.

brilliant recap

If we set effective goals in sales we are more likely to achieve the results that we want:

- Setting goals enables the brain to notice things that take you towards what you want to achieve.
- Brilliant salespeople set goals around their performance and specific situations such as meetings and what they want to achieve each day.
- Focus on setting goals around those things that you can control or influence.
- Break big goals down into smaller milestone goals to make them more motivating.
- Make sure goals are specific, measurable, achievable, relevant and time-bound.

CHAPTER 9

Managing sales information

I t may not be too much of a stretch to say that most salespeople did not get into selling to analyse data. Whilst selling has a lot to do with human interaction there is, however, an important role for data and for spending time understanding it, interpreting it and using it to improve our performance and results.

Data can often be an objective window into why we are achieving a certain result and a clue as to what to do about it. Without data you are not fully in control of your selling and may well only start to notice a potential problem when it is too late!

'The person who knows HOW will always have a job. The person who knows WHY will always be his boss.' – Diane Ravitch

What data should we pay attention to in sales?

This will vary depending on what you are selling, how you are selling it and to whom you are selling it, but there are some categories that are worth focusing on here.

- Data and information about what our market is doing. This might include trends, key issues, changes in how they do business, etc.

- Data and information on what specific prospects / customers are doing. How are they doing compared to their competition, what are their current issues, what does the annual report say, what is their revenue / margin with us this year compared to the last three years, etc.?

- Data and information on how other salespeople are doing within the company. What are their revenues, margins, pipeline figures, etc.?

- Data and information on how I am doing. Comparisons year on year, quarter on quarter around the important metrics against which my performance is judged.

How should we use it?

The first rule is to make sure you are objective about what the data are telling you. It is easy for us to read things into data that are based on our assumptions or what we want to believe. One great use for data is to help us form questions and hypotheses that we can then find ways to test. In testing these ideas we get more information upon which to base our sales decisions.

> make sure you are objective about what the data are telling you

Be sure to keep interpretation of data objective and relevant!

For example, if monthly sales data are showing that our average order value on a certain product is x and that this is 12% lower than half of our colleagues, we might do a number of things:

- Work out what a 12% increase would mean against the number of orders for that product, that we close in a month, in terms of increased revenues. This might give us the motivation to work on improving the figure.

- Look perhaps at sales data across all products for our colleagues, to see if there are any patterns; maybe other products with which they seem successful. This will give us a wider perspective for the data.

- Plan actions such as talking to colleagues about what they are doing relative to selling this particular product.

Sales pipeline data

The best salespeople manage their sales cycle – their pipeline. This pipeline management enables them to know more objectively if the relative activities and numbers in each stage of the pipeline are enough to achieve the result they need, whilst also eliminating peaks and troughs in sales, so that they can plan accordingly. They are disciplined and balanced in how and where they apply their time and effort.

> The best salespeople manage their sales cycle – their pipeline

A lot of companies have some form of system (either manual or based on a software application) that manages data on the sales pipeline. This can be very useful if used correctly. You might have access to data about the number of prospects at each stage of the sales cycle that can give you conversion rate information. You can use this by evaluating each step of the process and your performance, to get ideas as to where an improvement would make the most positive difference. Or you will be able to get empirical data about the number of prospects at each stage of your pipeline together with potential deal size, in order to help plan your activity and become aware of specific areas that you need to address.

Sales pipeline information differs dramatically but Brilliant Salespeople take the time to understand what the data are telling them and use it to inform their sales activities.

A pipeline often enables you to track the following information:

● Individual prospects: their name, the size of the deal, where they are in the cycle and the date it is likely to close.

● Sales forecast: maybe by week, month or quarter in terms of revenue or margin.

● Each stage of the sales cycle: showing the number of prospects at each stage and the value of possible deals at each stage.

● A percentage probability of the sale happening, to give a better idea of what the actual figures are likely to be. Sometimes this 'closing probability' is linked to each stage of the cycle. For example, if you are still qualifying the opportunity it may have a 20% probability, whereas if you are presenting the solution it might be a 60% probability.

brilliant tip

Email **resources@brilliant-selling.com** to receive a free resource pack with examples of sales pipeline forms.

⊿ brilliant recap

Sales information can be a real help in achieving results.

- We need to make time to look at the data – this brings objectivity to our planning and where we spend our time.
- Sales pipeline data are a strategic planning tool – and can help ensure that we achieve consistency to avoid 'feast or famine' results.
- We can use pipeline data to work out conversion rates and decide which activities in which we engage need more attention or development.

Used correctly, sales information helps us to avoid nasty surprises!

PART 3

Your power
to influence

I enjoy sport and many years ago I was looking forward to playing in an Easter hockey festival. A few days before the weekend I started getting pains in my stomach. The pain worsened and I ended up in hospital with appendicitis. After the operation and during the recovery phase, I got to know a fellow patient, Stanley Burns. He shared my passion for books and we became friends. One day in the hospital he was telling me about a time in his life when he traded jade in 1930s China. His story included an adventure with Somerset Maugham when he had appendicitis on the river Yangtze! I asked him: 'How were you, a Plymouth lad in your twenties and not well travelled, able to sell jade in China?' I remember his answer well – he said, 'It was simple really. At first I was no good at all and then I started thinking like a Chinese person – as soon as I started doing this, I began to be successful.'

We have all heard of the expression 'put yourself in the other person's shoes'. If you have a good sense of what the other wants, can think like the person you want to influence, behave and respect the person, then your chances of sales success increase dramatically. The core question is – how do you do that?

In this section, we are concerned with ethical influencing in sales situations. The key here is your objective – if you are trying to manipulate for a quick gain you can, potentially, use many unethical behaviours. However, if you believe there is a match between your service / product and what a customer wants, then of course you want to influence. The reality is that you are always influencing, whether you like it or not. The central questions are – do you know what effect you are having and are you making conscious choices about how you are influencing your prospects and customers?

There are some fundamentals that have to be in place if we want to get people to buy from us – whatever sales scenario or market we operate in. This chapter will cover some of these fundamentals and provide you with key information, which will allow you to influence people easily, both in your professional and personal lives.

Here are some questions at the heart of this influencing section that will be addressed:

- How do we influence the modern buyer?
- What needs to be in place for someone to be influenced?
- How do we consistently get into a positive state to influence well?
- What sort of questions will make the biggest difference?
- How can we demonstrate that we are actively paying attention to a buyer?
- How do we negotiate effectively and get an agreement that works?

CHAPTER 10

Credibility and rapport – the foundations of effective influencing

nfluencing is about producing an effect on an individual or group by imperceptible or intangible means. It is about shaping and determining a response, which will be linked to your outcome. Influencing done well is, of course, closely linked to persuasion, which is the process of changing attitudes, beliefs and opinions.

We often think of influencing in a negative sense and have a rather sensible approach in the UK: buyer beware. The reality is that we are influenced at a conscious and unconscious level all the time – through the people with whom we interact, and, of course, via marketing and advertising. Do you really think you are making completely conscious buying decisions when you are in the supermarket?

> we are influenced at a conscious and unconscious level all the time

'Influence may be the highest level of human skills' – Anon

Just consider this for a moment – think of a time in the last six months when you wanted to buy something. You did not need to be persuaded about a product, the price was acceptable and you walked into a store but left without buying the product. If this has ever happened to you, there is a good chance that the person serving influenced you NOT to buy! The salesperson may have done one (or more) of the following:

- Confused you with feature overload.
- Did not listen to what you wanted.
- Ignored you.
- Did not ask you any questions.
- Asked you what you perceived as an annoying question.
- Did not have the exact information you wanted.

Evidence suggests that, given a scenario like this, many people are prepared to pay more for exactly the same service or product from down the road or online.

Maybe you have also had the experience where you bought something from someone you really liked and then suffered from buyer's remorse at some stage after the sale had taken place, as you realised you did not really need what you had bought.

What is going on here? Well, what is happening is that you are being affected by the two foundations of influencing – credibility and rapport. Let me explain. In most sales situations it is unlikely that anyone will buy anything off a salesperson unless she has demonstrated credibility and built rapport. In your own sales scenarios you possibly already achieve this – otherwise you are unlikely to motivate people to buy. But do you know how to do this consciously and at will?

Establish credibility

Credibility derives from the Latin 'credo' which means 'I believe'. You need to be believable to sell. Indeed buyers are sorting for this when they meet you. What does this mean in practice? Here are ten top tips to establish credibility when selling:

1   Acquire as much knowledge as possible: of the customer, product / service, market and the competition.

2   Add value – all the time! At every meeting. Before any
    meeting ask yourself – what can I tell them that they do not
    already know? Think about how websites work well – there
    is often a huge amount of content given away free, which
    will work on establishing loyalty from the user.

3   Prepare effectively: set the agenda, define an outcome, do
    the research, think what questions the buyer is going to ask.

4   Execute efficiently: do what you say you are going to do.
    Under-promise and over-deliver, keep your word, be
    consistent, follow through and make clear agreements that
    are measurable.

5   Establish multiple links into the organisation: get an
    organisational chart, network, meet people, and get
    yourself known.

6   Avoid 'selling' too early: ask questions and listen first.

7   Take responsibility: we once worked with an organisation
    where there was a 'they' culture, as in 'they' were the
    internal people who did not support the sales team
    sufficiently well. You are your company, so speak about 'us'
    and 'we' and take responsibility for mistakes.

8   Present with enthusiasm: whether it is formally or
    informally, present sales materials with passion.

9   Make your buyers feel special: Do you know why people
    stop buying? The reasons are:

    1% die.

    3% move away.

    5% follow a friend's or relative's recommendation.

    9% find an alternative they perceive to be better quality or
    value.

    14% are dissatisfied with the product / service.

    And a massive 68% of people leave a business because of
    … indifference. They take their business elsewhere simply
    because they do not feel valued.

10   Have the courage to say no: they will respect you. Salespeople often say yes when they mean no and then have to
backtrack!

Build rapport

*'Paul is the most generous man with whom I've ever worked. We had a fantastic **rapport** shooting* Butch Cassidy. *It was one of the happiest experiences of my life'* – Robert Redford (1972 comment on Paul Newman)

Credibility comes first in selling, followed closely by rapport.

 brilliant definition

'Rapport is a harmonious connection with another person, which often takes place outside conscious awareness.'

Credibility comes first in selling, followed closely by rapport

It is about connectivity, getting on the same wavelength. Rapport is the naturally occurring dance that happens when people meet. Sometimes rapport occurs spontaneously. However, there are specific skills you can learn that enhance rapport and increase your effectiveness as a communicator and salesperson in business situations.

We have a natural rapport with friends and family, and in selling, rapport is the ability to relate to others in a way that creates a climate of trust and understanding. People generally do not buy from people they do not like.

exercise

Think of a recent face-to-face purchase when you bought something. Now think about a time when you did not buy – what are the distinctions in terms of rapport? What do you notice?

Rapport when I bought	Rapport when I did not buy

People have a tough time trusting salespeople with their time, money and business. Many people will not even want to talk to you. Welcome to reality! Your customers and prospects are busy and may feel that speaking with you is a waste of time. Many of your prospects may not even see a need for your product, or may be content with the version they already have. So, if you decide rapport is a good thing, you will have to build it quickly.

It could be argued that the rapport element has been over-played in sales training over the years, especially with the use of NLP (Neuro-Linguistic Programming), so that most salespeople understand its importance in the sales process. However, establishing and building rapport is a simple first step to show you are genuinely interested, and can act as a bridge to a mutually beneficial relationship. It depends on what you do, say and notice. Sometimes we meet people we do not like, but in selling if they do not warm to you they will start putting up barriers and the bridge can become a drawbridge!

brilliant tips

Here are ten top tips to establish and build rapport:

1   **Lobby in advance**: telephone and email someone so you build the connection early.

2   **Do the chit chat**: generally speaking, we tend not to dive straight into the business conversation. I was once training some business people from Brazil and they were telling me that it is thought rude in their country if you do not do what we describe as the 'small talk' in the UK for at least 45 minutes!

Avoid 'so, how's business?' – it might be terrible right now and get you off on the wrong footing!

3   **Share personal information** and find out more about their other interests: find out what makes them tick. People are 1,000 times more interested in themselves than they are in you (or your product or service). When you have discovered things –

holiday destinations, birthday, hobbies etc – remember and use the details.

4   People buy from people who are like themselves: **be like them**. You do this by closely identifying how they move, and speak and then copy them subtly. This idea is called matching and mirroring – see pages 112–114 for more information.

5   **Listen, listen, listen**: and then listen some more.

6   **Ask questions**: it shows you are interested and following the thoughts of the buyer.

7   **Look as though you are interested**: demonstrate curiosity through attentive body language, e.g. smile, nod or grunt!

8   **Be friendly**: I was in an audience recently and was amazed at the easy and straightforward way that the speaker lost his audience by being deliberately provocative and unfriendly.

9   **Lighten up and laugh**: Nothing is more powerful than humour when it comes to building rapport quickly. Laughter is the spark that can ignite interest and cordiality between you and the person you are influencing; it is hard to laugh with a person and not feel comfortable around them. Some salespeople take their job far too seriously! So, lighten up! If you make them laugh, they may just buy!

10   **Finally – get to the point!** State your objective and why they should listen. Avoid clichéd and insincere reasons like saving money, increasing productivity, and other transparent and ineffective reasons they have heard from many salespeople before you. Prospects and buyers do not enjoy wasting time by playing games.

For those of you who have not heard of matching and mirroring, here is a quick explanation.

Match and mirror

We were approached a couple of years ago by a health company focusing on NHS trusts. It so happened that the CEO called us on the telephone in our office. They had found our business, RTP (www.rtpc.co.uk), on the web. This is usually pot luck and means he will have called a number of other businesses. The CEO was worried about some disharmony on the board and was looking to do some team work training for this group. I asked what he was looking for from a consultancy and he used the word 'rigorous' quite a few times. I called Tom and suggested he take the opportunity. Sure enough, when he spoke to the guy, the same word was used. We decided to include the word five times in the proposal. Well, we won the work and I sent an email asking for the reason he had chosen us. I still have his response – 'we felt you had a very **rigorous** approach to helping us develop the board'. Now of course there were other factors, but we certainly spoke his language!

Matching and mirroring is a tool introduced to the world by Richard Bandler and John Grinder of NLP fame (Neuro-Linguistic Programming). They modelled Milton Erickson, a leading psychotherapist in the US and noticed that Erickson was outstanding at building rapport with his patients. Rapport building is based around the idea of pacing the person you are attempting to influence. Pacing is about putting yourself in the shoes of the other person. See the situation from where the other party is sitting...

- Why are they raising the issues they are?
- What constraints do they have?
- What pressures are they under?
- How do they think?
- What do they want?

Rapport is a way of demonstrating that you are like the other party. People tend to buy from people who are like them. As a rule we most prefer to say yes to the requests of people we know and like. The liking rule produces assent. So, if you match and mirror you will seem to be similar. The art is to do it in a subtle way – copying some aspect of their behaviour, which, done well, can bring about the 'harmonious connection'. Done badly or incongruously, of course, it can be annoying! So if the buyer has an unusual physical tic, please do not match this!

You can match another person using all the three communication channels when you sell – the visual, the verbal and the voice. This is how you do it:

Communication channel	What you can match
The visual (body language)	Posture Gestures Breathing Energy level Facial expressions
The verbal (what they say)	Specific language patterns (e.g. rigorous) Beliefs (see Part 1) Values (see Part 1) Humour Common interests
The voice (how they say what they say)	Tonality Rhythm Speed Volume

metaphor

Flying high

Often when you get on an aeroplane the first person you will hear is the captain, as in – 'Welcome aboard. My name is Captain Cassell . . .' At some point you will also hear the flight attendant. Next time you are on a plane, listen carefully to the way they speak. You may well notice these differences in their voices:

Captain – vocal qualities	Flight attendant – vocal qualities
Slow	Fast
Intonation goes down at the end of the sentence or phrase	Intonation goes up at the end of the sentence or phrase
Use pauses	Use few pauses
Short, clipped sentences	Long, possibly rambling sentences
Monosyllabic	Lots of variety and musicality in the voice

Essentially the captain uses a 'credible' voice pattern, whilst the flight attendant uses a 'rapport' voice. Think Barack Obama or Tony Blair for credible voice and Stephen Fry or Dawn French for rapport voice. Use both voice patterns when you are trying to influence and focus on the credible voice pattern, when you discuss your service / product and when you want them to make a decision. For more information send an email to resources@brilliant-selling.com.

You always have the choice of matching or mismatching the other person. There are times when you need to break rapport. If someone is making a decision in a buying situation it may be appropriate momentarily to mismatch (the opposite of matching) him so he is making the decision himself.

🔎 brilliant recap

Without credibility and rapport with your prospects, customers and anyone else that you come into contact with in the selling process, you are going to have a tough time influencing and getting past first base. In this chapter the key areas that have been covered are:

- Credibility is built around knowledge (of your organisation, your customers' business and the market), preparation and execution.

- It is tough to be influenced by someone you do not like on some level – so find ways to ensure you are liked.

- Matching the customer is a simple and effective way of getting on the same wavelength and tuning in to the way that another is communicating.

- You can use the voice in different ways to establish credibility and build rapport.

So, there we have it – the twin pillars of effective influencing. There is one more element that needs to be there if you are to become a charismatic influencer: the ability to come across as confident and in control. So are you in control of your state?

CHAPTER 11

Managing your state – being confident whenever you want

I wonder if you have ever had this sort of experience – a day or part of a day when everything went right in your sales job – people said yes, there was an ease in the way you dealt with any problems and you got a huge kick out of all your interactions. You may have experienced what positive psychologist Mihály Csíkszentmihályi calls a 'flow state' either in a sales role or another job or activity. This is a mental state of operation in which you are fully involved in an experience. We have other terms for this – 'in the zone', 'on the ball', 'really with it' – a time when there is focus and absorption in the task, a balance between ability level and challenge in an activity, which is intrinsically rewarding. This sort of positive state or a lighter version of this state is a great way to be when we are selling or influencing others. But do you have any idea how to access this state at will? If you want to find out more, then this chapter is for you.

'Even when I was in the orphanage, when I was roaming the street trying to find enough to eat, even then I thought of myself as the greatest actor in the world. I had to feel the exuberance that comes from utter confidence in yourself. Without it, you go down to defeat.' – Charlie Chaplin, actor and film director

What is a state?

The state you are in will affect everything else going on in you and around you. But, what exactly is a state?

 brilliant definition

A state is the way you are feeling at a given moment – a combination of thought, emotion and physiology. It combines our mental pictures, sounds and feelings, physical energy and breathing.

We often think of a state in a negative way as in 'he's in a right state' or 'she's got out of bed the wrong side today'. We go through many different states in any single day. You may, at times, be happy, sad, depressed, nervous, excited or energised.

Nowadays many top sports people use sports psychologists to help train them mentally to win. It is part of their routine. Why? Because it works! Accessing the right state is critical to being at your best when you sell. When you are feeling really good about yourself, and confident, you will sell well. Things going on inside us affect the success of any sales performance. The state we are in impacts on our physiology, affecting our behaviour – which is what your client or prospect will see when you are selling. State management is the ability to choose the most appropriate state at any given moment. So, take a moment to define how to do this easily ....

 brilliant exercise

What sort of state do you want to be in when you sell?

Decide the state you would ideally like to be in when you sell to both prospects and existing customers. What name would you give to this state?

How do I get into this resourceful selling state?

So you now know your ideal selling state – confident, relaxed, focused, or what ever you have chosen. Can you get into this state at will? Are you secretary of your own state? Or do you allow others to affect your state?

📐 brilliant exercise

Here are the steps to get into a resourceful state:

1 Recall a time when you were in your desired state.

2 Either look up towards your left, or close your eyes, and go back into that time now and remember what you saw, heard and felt – make sure you see a picture, through your own eyes, that is a movie, in full colour and you can see the picture easily.

3 Now notice how it makes you feel in the present. Many people start feeling the state. When this happens, know that you can repeat this process and access this state whenever you want.

Here are some additional ideas about accessing a state that will allow you to sell at peak performance:

- Get physiologically comfortable – get balanced.
- Get your breathing under control – 5 deep breaths held for 5 seconds will usually do it, deep into your diaphragm.
- Concentrate on a spot in your line of sight and expand your awareness to your peripheral vision. Allow yourself just to relax.

Being in a resourceful state leads inexorably to what most of us think of as a positive attitude. Our Brilliant Selling survey (**www.brilliant-selling.com**) reveals that top salespeople understand the importance of attitude in selling. Indeed, asked

top salespeople understand the importance of attitude in selling

to choose whether attitude or skill was more important, 77% said attitude. This positive attitude is also likely to be there for you if you decide on a successful outcome for every major meeting. What will good look like? Imagine what it will be like to progress or take the order. What would you see, hear and feel? I remember when I was working for a big corporate and they offered a new Mini car as a first prize for a new product launch. I immediately imagined myself winning the car and walking up to collect the key on stage. Partly because I created such a vivid picture in my mind, I literally drove myself to succeed and it was quite a feeling when I strode up and took possession of the vehicle.

spend some time remembering a positive event

brilliant recap

So, we do have control of our state and it is a bedrock of successful salespeople. You do not necessarily have to go as far as Tom Cruise in *Jerry Maguire* when he shouted 'show me the money' to change his state but you can spend some time remembering a positive event and then allowing yourself to sell confidently, every time.

Here are the key areas that have been covered in this chapter:

● Accessing the right state is critical to being at your best when you sell.

● You can become secretary of your own state.

● In our Brilliant Selling Survey 77% said attitude was more important than skill.

CHAPTER 12

Asking the right questions

When I was learning to be a coach my trainer told me that 'questions are the answer'. It is much the same with selling. You cannot sell well without gathering information and it is tough to gather information without asking questions. Yet, according to a study by the Sales Career Training Institute, salespeople typically spend too much time pitching and not enough time asking the right questions so that they can discover the prospect's / buyer's real concerns and issues, as well as the hot buttons they need to press to get someone to buy.

'Judge others by their questions rather than by their answers.' – Voltaire

So, what are the benefits of asking the right questions?

- By asking the right questions you will demonstrate that you are interested, rather than being focused on making a sale. This will increase the likelihood that the prospect / buyer will open up and that rapport will start to build.
- You will identify what really matters and what the core issues are that you can help to address.
- It gives you an element of control.
- It creates momentum, which is one of the core goals of every sales conversation.
- Questions encourage emotional involvement.

Here are 7 core principles that will guide you to ask the right questions:

1   **Start with an attitude of curiosity**

    Any salesperson used to a consultative approach will use questions naturally. Asking intelligent questions comes from an attitude of curiosity. Think about it – you are on a 'quest' for information. Anyone who has kids knows that if they are curious about something they will quite naturally ask questions.

    Curiosity is infectious. You will soon find the person you are influencing becomes curious about his / her own situation!

    'The important thing is not to stop questioning. Curiosity has its own reason for existing.' – Albert Einstein

2   **Have a clear outcome for your questions**

    Ask yourself: what am I trying to achieve by asking questions? This avoids asking unnecessary or random questions.

3   **Let the conversation flow naturally**

    Good questioning techniques do not mean that you become an interrogator. Avoid the clipboard approach.

    > Avoid the clipboard approach

4   **Use both open and closed questions**

    Open questions start with who, why, what, how, where and when.

    Closed questions elicit a yes / no answer.

    There is no evidence that we have ever seen that open questions are more successful in making a sale. However, it is likely that you will start with OPEN questions to elicit information and there will be more open questions in a typical sales conversation. Use CLOSED questions for clarification and agreement.

5 Make your questions understandable

I have heard many a sales question that is frankly unintelligible. Sometimes people use multiple questions, or ask a question and then answer it themselves, or ask a question which has no real link to what is being discussed. Make sales questions straightforward to understand – often the simple questions are the most powerful. Such as:

> often the simple questions are the most powerful

- What do you want?
- What are your key priorities?
- What is really going to make the difference?
- What is working for you?

6 Ask questions that help you pinpoint the dominant buying motivations

Buying motivations and specific needs are not always the same. Buying motivations are about desires and feelings – they are more emotional and intangible.

You can find out what motivates your buyer – what he wants – by asking simple questions such as: 'What kind of similar products or services have you bought in the past?'

The knowledge you gain will tell you what benefits to emphasise.

7 Avoid offending your buyers!

Some questions can offend a prospect and cause them to reject you and your ideas.

Avoid leading or 'setup' questions such as, 'You do want your children to have a fair chance, don't you?' What is the prospect going to say? 'No! It's a tough world – let them sink or swim!'

Nosey, gossipy or overly personal questions can be a real turnoff. Stick to business!

Sometimes your manner can be threatening. Instead of asking, 'How much do you want to spend?' why not phrase it, 'How much had you planned to invest?'

So – what areas of questioning are most useful?

'If you are not moving closer to what you want in sales (or in life), you probably aren't doing enough asking.' – Jack Canfield, inspirational self-help author and success coach

Research suggests that you will make the most impact if you focus your questioning around these nine areas:

1 **Needs and wants**
   This is absolutely central to the role of the salesperson. Find out more about specific questions that elicit needs and wants by reading the chapter 'Identifying what the prospect wants and needs'.

2 **Ask the buyer for selection criteria**
   This is often avoided in sales, so take the initiative and find out who your contact is dealing with right now and who else he / she might be considering. This will elicit the buyer's criteria and values and will help you align your service / product with what the organisation wants.

   The more you can align the values of the buyer with what you can provide in terms of service and delivery, the more you are likely to build a long-term relationship. I had a colleague once who was even more upfront. He used to ask: 'What can I do to win your business?'

   'Selling' is closely linked in meaning to 'serving'. The founder of a client of ours, Sodexo, based his whole strategy on the maxim – 'true dignity lies in being of service to others'. How can you be 'of service to others' unless you know how they like to be served?

Here are some questions you might consider:

- What's important in your commercial relationships with suppliers?
- How do you choose your current suppliers?
- How do you decide with whom to do business?
- What do you really value in a salesperson?

↗ brilliant exercise

Think about your own context. What other questions are there that would work well for you?

3 **Options**

Discover what options they are considering. If they are still at the options stage you can influence their decision making.

Here are some questions you might consider:

- What sort of options are you looking for?
- Who are we up against?
- Who else will you be speaking with in regard to this decision?
- What have you been considering?

↗ brilliant exercise

Think about your own context. What other questions are there that would work well for you?

4 **Your service / product**

You need to gauge the reaction to your service / product to find out if they are likely to buy and what more information they need to make a decision.

Here are some questions you might consider:

- What are your expectations / requirements for this product / service?

- Have you seen anything else on the market that you especially do not like?

- What further information do you need right now?

- If you do decide to go ahead, what sort of consequences will this have?

---

 brilliant exercise

Think about your own context. What other questions are there that would work well for you?

---

5 **People**

Often a buying decision for an organisation will have implications for many people. We sell training, coaching and consultancy services at RTP (www.rtpc.co.uk) and the people who could be implicated by any decision to use us could include sales, HR, Operations, marketing, senior management and the board.

Here are some questions you might consider:

- Who will be involved if we progress to the next stage?

- How will people's roles change if you decide to take this product / service?

- Who will be involved in the roll-out?
- What obstacles might be in the way of moving this forward?

 exercise

Think about your own context. What other questions are there that would work well for you?

6 Decision making

I remember that I once had three meetings with someone and focused quite a lot of time and energy on the opportunity, before finding out that this person was not the decision maker. Have you ever done something similar? Find out what the decision-making process is and who is involved. This will allow you to focus your energy.

Here are some questions you might consider:

- What can you tell me about your decision-making process?
- Who is the key decision maker within the business?
- How can we help support you internally?
- How much support does this have at the executive level?

 exercise

Think about your own context. What other questions are there that would work well for you?

7 **Budget**

There may or may not be a budget for your offering. It is really helpful to know what amount has been budgeted and with what timescale. When qualifying, assess where a prospect is in their buying cycle. They need to be injected into the sales process at the right point. So many salespeople ignore the customer buying cycle and just enforce a rigid sales cycle, and wonder why they fail.

We were able once to do a deal with an organisation (later to become a key account) in which they used their budget for the following year and we invoiced them at a later date. They appreciated our flexibility!

Here are some questions you might consider

● How do you handle budget considerations?

● What price range you are considering?

● Who is paying for this?

● How will the funding for the project be justified?

 brilliant exercise

Think about your own context. What other questions are there that would work well for you?

8 **Momentum / qualifying**

Salespeople spend too long sometimes talking to prospects when there is little hope of the prospect buying and where there is no momentum. Ask qualifying questions to establish whether this opportunity is worth pursuing.

Here are some questions you might consider:

● What do you see as the next action steps?

- What is your timeline for implementing / purchasing this type of service / product?
- What constraints do you have in this area?
- What further information do we need to discuss before we move this forward?

 exercise

Think about your own context. What other questions are there that would work well for you?

9   **Extending the relationship**

Of course questions do not stop when the prospect becomes a customer. Keep on asking questions. If they are delighted by you and your service then ask questions which will allow you to extend the relationship or cross-sell. Or ask them to give you a referral – people will happily do this if they like the product / service and like you!

> Ask for referrals at the height of the gratitude curve

Ask for referrals at the height of the gratitude curve – when they think you are great and have offered an outstanding service.

Here are some questions you might consider:

- What else are you looking to address in the business right now or in the future?
- What other opportunities are there within the business?
- Would it be helpful for you to know what else we offer?
- Who else do you know in business who might like what we have to offer?

↗ brilliant exercise

Think about your own context. What other questions are there that would work well for you?

↗ brilliant recap

So, it is not just about asking random questions in order to tease out answers. Brilliant Selling needs to be focused on asking the right questions at the right time to the right person. Successful salespeople use similar skills in this area to a top business coach – they ask questions that:

- are understandable and logical
- work to help the buyer get clarity
- build momentum.

So, take your time before each sales meeting you have in the future and ask yourself which questions are most appropriate and notice that questions are the answer to developing a better understanding of the people you want to influence. The key points from this section are:

- There are 7 principles – be curious, have an outcome, let the conversation flow, use open and closed questions, make your questions understandable, identify motivations and avoid offending your buyers.
- Ask focused questions to identify needs and wants, options, reaction to your product / service, decision making, budget, qualification and extending the relationship.

And of course questions are only half of it. If you cannot listen well then you will reduce rapport and be unable to take the customer to the next stage...

CHAPTER 13

Listening and learning

So, honestly, how good are you at listening? It is almost a cliché that listening is a core sales skill, and yet it is surprising how often salespeople are not primarily focused on listening when they sell. Time and again research suggests that those who really listen tend to be more successful in developing long-term relationships (in selling and life in general!).

'The reason why God gave us two ears and one mouth is so that we may listen more and talk less.' – Diogenes

 brilliant exercise

Listening limiters

The following list contains some of the common reasons why salespeople end up *not* listening when selling, or giving the impression of not listening. Have you ever caught yourself thinking them, doing them or saying them, while someone has been speaking to you? They are **listening limiters** and will detract from your effectiveness as a salesperson.

What are your dark and guilty secrets? Tick any of these 15 where you must plead guilty. And, come on, be honest with yourself!

( ) Rehearsing what I am going to say about my product / service while the other person is still talking.

( ) Getting impatient for them to finish so I can start talking.

▶

( ) Not being interested in what they are trying to communicate.

( ) Getting bored and thinking about something else (football, cars, children, what you did last night, holidays, what's your specialty?) while they are speaking.

( ) Thinking 'I'm a busy person' – I have got so many other things I could be getting on with.

( ) Tapping on my computer keyboard when on the telephone to clients or prospects.

( ) Anticipating what they are going to say before they say it.

( ) Dismissing what they are saying as irrelevant to me.

( ) Finishing off other people's sentences, talking over the other person or interrupting.

( ) Thinking that they are making the point far too slowly to keep me interested.

( ) Thinking, 'Who cares what they are concerned about? I have got my own worries to deal with!'

( ) Preferring to talk rather than keep quiet.

( ) Assuming that they do not know what they are talking about before they speak.

( ) Fidgeting and appearing not to be listening.

( ) Focusing on something else in the room and losing focus.

If you have scored six or more, then this chapter is for you! Brilliant listeners put aside these distractions and really listen. If you are curious you will listen and if you are really focused on the other party and minimise distractions, you can listen with rapt attention.

The benefits can be extraordinary. People open up, they indicate how they like to receive information, they confide in you, they speak about the most interesting and important person in their worlds – themselves!

Listening should be an active process in selling and, if you develop this muscle, you will improve your ability to influence others. There are eight elements of active listening:

> Listening should be an active process in selling

1 Value the other party: show concern and demonstrate that you respect his / her position.

2 Listen to what is not said: pay attention to what is missing, beliefs masked as judgements and body language.

3 Limit the time you speak: many people have low attention spans. Salespeople talk too much – so, minimise your chunks of 'sales speak' to about 30 seconds. You may have heard of the 'power of 3' before. Three is a magical number and if you limit yourself to three key points you will come across with more credibility.

4 Avoid thinking about what you are about to say: you will miss the message. Do not try and manipulate the conversation by asking questions to which you already know the answer.

5 Listen to the other party's point of view: she has a unique perception of the world.

6 Repeat and reflect the other's comments to ensure you heard them correctly, or summarise.

7 Take notes: but avoid transcripts.

8 Maintain eye contact whenever possible.

> Repeat and reflect the other's comments

Because this area is so critical, here is a comparison of what characterises good and bad listeners.

Good listeners	Bad listeners
React non-verbally, with a smile, a nod or a frown as appropriate.	Interrupt frequently and jump to conclusions without waiting for the whole message.
Ask questions for clarification.	
Re-state or paraphrase some of the speaker's words to show understanding.	Are so busy formulating their replies that they do not listen to the speaker.
Display empathy by acknowledging feelings.	Let their thoughts take excursions while the other person is speaking.
Make regular eye contact with the speaker.	Get distracted by details.
Pay close attention and do not let their minds wander.	Stop listening when the subject matter gets difficult.
	Only listen for what they like to hear.
Use their thought speed to analyse, sort and store material.	Let their emotions take over.

�

brilliant recap

Remember the old adage – we have two ears and one mouth, so use them in that proportion when you sell. Listening really can make a huge difference in building relationships, avoiding misunderstanding and ensuring you hear what your buyers want.

Remember:

● Listening well gets people to open up and they confide in you.

● To reduce listening limiters and focus your attention.

● Listening is an active process, so demonstrate your interest.

Brilliant listeners can also be Brilliant negotiators, so let's continue our influencing journey by identifying how to negotiate and create win–wins with our buyers.

CHAPTER 14

Negotiating collaboratively

Negotiation is not selling. Equally, you do not necessarily have to negotiate when you sell. Selling is about persuading and convincing. Negotiation is about tying up the loose ends.

The mistake that many salespeople make is that they assume that negotiation is inevitable. I was once buying a second-hand car, and liked the look of a particular one advertised locally. I called the seller and he asked me to come around. Now I do not know much about cars but my ears pricked up when I asked him the price. He said, '£5,500, but I am open to negotiation.' He made an elementary error – he gave away that price immediately. Do you think I paid £5,500? No, of course not. What he should have done was to sell me on the car – housed in a garage, regular service history, the fact he had been the only owner, and so on. But he was too worried about the price he wanted to achieve. Unsurprisingly, I was able to negotiate a much better price!

During the house boom of early 2002 my friend had a house for sale at £325,000. He had a number of people interested and was called one morning by the estate agent who said 'Mr and Mrs Stevens are really interested in the house. They would like to offer £315,000, although they are prepared to go to the full asking price if necessary.' Can you imagine my friend's response?

Commercially, a salesperson presents a proposal to a customer. The customer may accept every point in the proposal and a contract is signed. In this situation, no negotiation has taken place. However, if the customer does not accept certain aspects of the proposal, there is an initial position of non-agreement. At this point, a negotiation is required to reach an agreement. Equally, there is no point in a purchasing manager negotiating with a supplier until he is certain that the product / service meets his requirements. To take a non-purchasing / selling example, it is unwise for a recruitment manager to negotiate on salary with a potential employee, until it is established that the person is right for the job. Negotiation, then, is about agreeing the conditions with another party (or parties) under which you will do business together.

'He who has learned to disagree without being disagreeable has discovered the most valuable secret of a diplomat.' – Robert Estabrook, Editor and foreign correspondent, *Washington Post*.

Most often you will be negotiating at the back of the sales process once the buyer has decided there is a potential match between what he wants and what you can deliver. However, whenever there is a position of non-agreement you may have to negotiate. These scenarios may include speaking to or meeting the ultimate decision maker or meeting other interested parties in the organisation.

Negotiation principles

If you start applying these five core principles whenever you are involved in a negotiation, you will improve your results:

1 **Work to a win-win**

'I will work with them on reaching an agreement with which we are all comfortable.'

A long-term business relationship can only work on this collaborative basis. Collaborate comes from the Latin 'com laborare', which means 'work with.'

In buying and selling terms, the sellers feel that they are receiving appropriate 'revenue' for the service that they are providing. The purchasers feel that they are receiving value.

2 **Decide optimum and fallback positions**

In any situation we have our ideal, i.e., the best that we can get from an agreement. This is the optimum. However, implicit in any collaborative negotiation is preparedness to look at the variables, and the 'reshaping' of an original proposition. This **may** involve moving from an ideal situation to something less than ideal, but which is still acceptable to you and the other parties. This is the fallback.

The area between two parties' optimum and fallback positions is the negotiation window, the window of opportunity to reach an agreement...

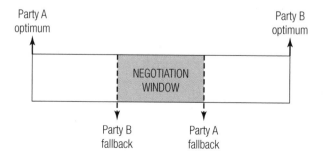

The proposal you put to a customer must be the proposal you believe the customer will buy. It represents your optimum position or just above your optimum.

If you signal: 'This is my proposition but I am prepared to negotiate', it will result in a negotiation!

There is a difference between having calculated your fallback and being prepared to negotiate, if necessary, and **assuming** that you will have to negotiate.

3   Trade concessions

Negotiation often involves conceding, moving from your original position. Fundamental to collaborative sales negotiation is concession exchanging, or not giving.

> Negotiation often involves conceding

Salespeople have the tendency to cave in when faced with issues around a price or fees. You need to remind yourself of this give and take principle; a concession (e.g. reduce the price) which involves a cost needs to be balanced by something received which has a value (e.g. extra volume).

Reciprocity is at the heart of what we as humans do, so this principle works well. It permeates much of the exchanges in the sales process. Have you ever had the experience when you were offered a free sample in a supermarket and felt obliged to buy? Robert Cialdini in his seminal book 'Influence' tells the story of:

'... a university professor who tried a little experiment. He sent Christmas cards to a sample of perfect strangers ... the response he received was amazing – holiday cards addressed to him came pouring back from people who had never met nor heard of him (Kunz and Walcott, 1976).'

Costs and values are not always in straightforward financial terms.

Setting up an exchange process is key to effective negotiation, for example:

A purchaser may request

| • Discounts
• Special credit terms
• Preferential service | *In exchange a seller may request* | • Extra volume
• Additional opportunities
• Long-term commitment |

4 Work on all the variables

In selling, there is a danger that price / discount become the focus point in any negotiation. Working on all of the variables involves taking a broader view, considering a number of ways to get to an agreement.

'Any business arrangement that is not profitable to the other person will in the end prove unprofitable for you. The bargain that yields mutual satisfaction is the only one that is apt to be repeated.'
– BC Forbes, founder of *Forbes* magazine

An open atmosphere will lead to a positive meeting. Exploring possibilities, generating ideas will assist in building cooperation. The more ideas on the table, the greater the possibilities of an agreement being reached, acceptable to all parties.

'I believe that there are a number of ways to approach this ...'

'I have a couple of ideas that may help. Can I ...'

'Maybe we could look at ...'

'I see two clear ways of providing you with ...'

'I think that I can see some solutions ...'

'What options are there ...?'

Remember, by suggesting you are not committing. Keep the discussion open.

5 Avoid assumptions

Salespeople can be guilty of assumptions or mind reading that bears little relation to what is really happening. Always test assumptions, if you can. Avoid these typical assumptions:

- The same people who were there at the last meeting will be there at the next meeting.
- They are bound to haggle on price.
- All the key people have read the proposal.
- There is nothing for you to offer as a trade.

We were guilty of making assumptions very recently. We walked into a fourth meeting with a prospect, thinking that we might have to negotiate on fees and terms. However, the prospect wheeled out three new big hitters and they spent over an hour grilling us on our proposal. We had to move swiftly back from negotiating to persuading! Fortunately we still won the work, but it reminded us of this important principle.

> Always test assumptions, if you can

Negotiation tactics

In your everyday life you cannot not negotiate – you do it every day with your family, friends, colleagues and in shops and on the telephone. But what sort of tactics do you use? Are you aware of the ones that really make the difference? Here are seven tactics which you can use in sales negotiations that will sharpen your negotiation skills and allow you to get a better deal for you and your organisation.

1 Build debt

If the other party has negotiated a point that is close to, or at, your fallback position you may wish to let them know the significance of the concession they have just received.

This can be used at a later stage of the meeting to secure concessions in your favour, or to fend off other demands!

'We can agree to ... in this case, as we can see the benefits of building long-term business with you. I must stress though that this payment schedule does represent ...'

This need not be confrontational.

2   Consistency

People, generally, will act in a consistent way and you can use that to your advantage. For example, appealing for help, when used consciously to relationship build and / or generate new ideas, is a potentially powerful behaviour. Of course, it depends on a positive relationship having been developed in previous meetings.

3   Use standards and objective criteria

This can help to provide a rationale for a position that is important to you. For example, as a seller:

● A customer may demand 60-day credit terms.

● Your standard terms are 30 days; at the most you could go to 45 days.

Saying to a customer 'Our terms are 30 days,' is merely reinforcing the difference in your positions.

If you can provide factual data that the industry standard is 30 days and this is the reason for the position you are taking, it helps show the logic of your case.

4   Summarise

Summarising is a positive behaviour during all stages of a meeting. The longer and more complex the topic, the greater the need to summarise. In the context of negotiation, summary is important in that it:

● Checks, clarifies, and avoids misunderstanding.

● Provides an opportunity, when a sticking point is reached, to emphasise the positive – what has already been achieved. It is therefore a motivator to continue, to reach an agreement ...

'I think that this may be a difficult point; however, let's just recap on what we have agreed so far. I believe it will put this point into context ...'

5 Defer

No matter how well you have planned any face-to-face or telephone meeting the unplanned 'sticking point' can always occur. The danger is that you never move on from that point. Deferring is a technique to move contentious issues to the end of the agenda, enabling other agreements to be made.

'I think that this subject could take us some time ... I suggest that we look at some of the other items first, and come back to this one later. Does that make sense?'

6 Adjourn

An adjournment can be for ten minutes, two days, or two weeks. Calling for an adjournment provides time to confer with colleagues, speak to your sales manager or carry out calculations, costings and implications. This 'breakout' can also help both parties see specific points in perspective. Much better to adjourn than accommodate and then have to backtrack at a later stage.

'We are getting into some detail. I suggest we break for 15 minutes, as I need to contact the office to clarify some specific points.'

7 The Flinch

The Flinch is a physical or verbal exclamation of surprise / horror at the ridiculous offer / price made by someone in a fee negotiation. Never accept the first offer, and flinch so you demonstrate that the offer is unacceptable. You can flinch big or small, and learn different flinches for different situations. I once worked with a negotiator who was able to summon tears in a heartbeat – a solitary tear rolling down a cheek is one of the more unusual flinches I have come across.

To find out the 30 specific questions you should be asking before you negotiate, email us at **resources@brilliant-selling.com**.

↗ brilliant recap

We have covered a fair amount of material on negotiation here. Let us just recap the key elements of this chapter. We have focused on:

- Treating negotiation as a separate part of the sales process.

- Recognising that negotiating is not inevitable.

- Five key principles: work to a win–win, have an optimum and fallback position, trade concessions, work on variables, avoid assumption.

- Seven tactics to sharpen your negotiating skills: build debt, consistency, standards and objective criteria, summarise, defer, adjourn, the flinch.

PART 4

Understanding buyers and prospects

It was the end of the third quarter. I was a few thousand pounds away from hitting my sales target. I had done well, but not well enough to hit my quarterly target and therefore a retrospective bonus. I surveyed my options – and it was not looking good. So I called some friends – three of my main accounts - and asked them to take an order right now for products they would need in the future. They all obliged and I hit my numbers. That was almost 20 years ago. In those days, and before then, you could survive in sales by using your native wit and by becoming friends with your customers. Nowadays, however, the sales environment has completely changed and we are met with complex sales scenarios, in which we deal with sophisticated, educated, well trained buyers or procurement specialists. The days of the handshake, the 'do us a favour' approach, are, largely, over. We are sometimes faced with ITTs (Invitations To Tender), panel decisions, and specific procurement selection criteria. There is much more rigour in the buying process and expectations have grown enormously about what organisations and buyers want from the salespeople who serve them.

This chapter considers these questions:

- What are some distinctions in sales approaches?
- Who is the modern buyer?
- What qualities does he want to see from salespeople?
- How do you get in front of buyers?
- How do you identify what the buyer needs and wants?

CHAPTER 15

How do you sell?

How do you and your organisation sell? What sort of approach do you employ? There are essentially two models of selling, and you and your business are likely to adopt the one that best fits your market. Here is a brief overview of the approaches.

Transactional selling

In transactional selling, the focus is on finding prospects with a requirement to develop relationships, focus on features and benefits and to take orders for the desired products or services at an acceptable price to all parties. The customers are likely to have a clear need for a 'standard' product or service and will be interested in sources that can provide it at the right time and at an acceptable price.

> In transactional selling, customers are likely to need a 'standard' product / service

Consultative (or solution/relationship) selling

In consultative, solution or relationship selling (all synonyms), the salesperson develops a greater understanding of the challenges faced by the customer and there is likely to be a tailored solution. Questioning and listening become more important than communicating features and positioning statements.

In consultative selling there is likely to be a tailored solution.

The actual purchase decision is often managed through a proposal, contract negotiation and solution delivery. The consultative selling approach is much more common nowadays and is most appropriate for businesses that offer a transformational product or service such as consulting or specialised, rarely purchased items. Suppliers of transformational products or services find consultative selling necessary, due to the customers' lack of understanding of the possibilities.

'Too many salespeople are "talking brochures", trying to show customers how their products or services are better than competitors. Salespeople must become value creators.' – Neil Rackham

Many organisations across the world have trained their sales teams to become business partners and adopt consultative selling strategies. If organisations implement the 'salesman as business partner' model successfully, there can be huge upsides. The benefits are that:

- It is more difficult for the competition to win business.
- It is possible to access decision makers higher up the food chain.
- Accounts can become more profitable in the long-term.
- There is a higher degree of job satisfaction from salespeople and this increases retention.

Overview of differences

	Transactional	Consultative
Type of sale	Standard / commodity	Strategic, often transformational
Current status	Less common because of e-commerce and procurement sophistication	More common because of increasing complexity of businesses and globalisation

	Transactional	Consultative
Salesperson	Telesales Web Order takers, sometimes face to face	Face to face Subject matter expert Problem solver
Sales cycle	Can be quick	Likely to take quite some time (often several meetings)
Knowledge	Customer probably knows what he wants	Customer open to education, probably does not know solution or even that there is a problem
Focus	Features and benefits	Matching needs with bespoke solutions
Sale	Small and many	Large and few
Price	Critical and central to buying decision	Collaborative and based around trading concessions
Prospecting	Critical and short-term	Important and slow-burn
Procurement department	Sometimes involved	Often involved
Relationship with buyer	Often short-term and transactional in nature	Likely to be long-term and collaborative

brilliant recap

In this short chapter we have identified:

- There are essentially two models of selling.

- Transactional selling is often used when there is a 'standard' product or service to sell.

- Consultative selling is focused on developing long-term relationships and is often used for selling bespoke solutions.

CHAPTER 16

The modern buyer

In order to understand how people responsible for corporate buying decisions feel about their interactions with salespeople, DDI (the selection and development specialists, **www.ddi world.com**) recently conducted a major global study of corporate buyers. Survey respondents included 2,705 corporate buyers and those involved with the buying process across six countries (Australia, Canada, France, Germany, the UK and US) and representative of a wide range of industries, job levels and age groups.

DDI specifically wanted to know how these people view their buyer–seller relationships and asked buyers a series of questions which included:

- What qualities do they value in a salesperson?
- Have their expectations of salespeople changed?
- What value do salespeople provide to buying organisations?

'He who buys need have 100 eyes, but one's enough for him that sells the stuff.' – Benjamin Franklin

 brilliant exercise

Take a moment to think of at least one of your current buyers.

1 Write down what you think they want out of the relationship between them and you and the business you represent.

2 Write down what you imagine they think of you.

Maybe you have written a glowing self-reference; and maybe that is fair. The stark reality is that what buyers really think about salespeople does not make particularly comfortable reading, according to this recent study.

many buyers have a poor perception of salespeople

The research suggested that many buyers have a poor perception of salespeople. Here are some of the comments from buyers about salespeople captured by the researchers:

- 'Unwilling to listen.'
- 'Won't take no for an answer.'
- 'Lacking knowledge about their products.'
- 'More interested in commission than what I need.'
- 'Doesn't understand my circumstances.'

Hardly a ringing endorsement!

The move away from transactional selling means that salespeople should be adding more value throughout the whole sales

Only 6% rated the sales profession 'excellent'

process. However, when buyers were asked to describe their perceptions of the sales process, the most common description, across all countries, was that the sales process is 'a necessary evil'. Only 6% rated the sales profession 'excellent'. Buyers in the UK provided the lowest ratings, with 53% rating sales 'Poor' or 'Fair'. Overall, 54% of buyers said 'Yes' to this question – would you consider your sales contacts business partners? So, over half are now getting more value from the relationship, although there were regional differences. In the UK for instance, only 42% answered 'Yes'.

There is a positive intent articulated by buyers. For example, more than 90% of customers would like their salesperson to be more of a resource to them. More worryingly perhaps is that over two-thirds of buyers believe salespeople's expertise is getting worse.

The key finding that stood out was this:

- 61% of buyers said sales representatives were transaction-orientated only and did not understand customer needs.

Whilst many organisations, sales managers and salespeople understand the necessity to reach beyond the transaction model, many buyers feel differently. The report highlights the growing gap between what buyers want from salespeople and what they are routinely given in terms of service and expertise.

So let us start looking at ways in which salespeople, across all market sectors and across the globe, can really make a difference. There *are* salespeople out there adding value, offering great service, aligning what they offer with their customers' requirements and making great money! Our survey of 200 salespeople (**www.brilliant-selling.com**) suggests that these people are open to change, flexible and thoroughly professional. They adapt their approach and meet the evolving needs of the people who make the decisions.

So what are the expectations of **the buyer**? What questions do they have as they decide which partners to choose? These are 20 key questions that are on buyers' minds:

Your offering

- What is your product / service?
- How does your product / service fit with my business and my current business outcomes?
- How will your product / service help me now and in the future?
- How can you guarantee the quality of your product or service?

Legitimacy of your business

- What sort of reputation does your company have?
- What experience does your company have in my market?
- What would others in my business think of your product / service?

Competition

- Why should I buy from you and not someone else?

Price versus value

- Why should I pay your price?
- Can I make sufficient margin by buying your product / service?

Timing

- Do I really need to buy this now?
- Can I wait to buy your product?
- What would be the implications if I did wait to buy?

You

- What relevant experience do you have in my market / business?
- What do first impressions tell me about you, your product / service and your company?
- What would others in my organisation think of you?
- Am I likely to trust you?
- How will you help me achieve my own personal goals?
- Do I like you?
- Can I see you as a potential business partner in the future?

Just as salespeople are paid on results, so, increasingly, are buyers. They have real fears that we need to identify and meet. These will include:

- The fear of paying too much.
- The fear of change.
- The fear of being left behind.
- The fear of loss.

Our job as a salesperson is to answer the buyers' questions and address their fears. And so the ultimate question for any buyer is:

'Why should I buy from you?'

There is plenty of competition out there and, if we are not able to answer this basic question, with a degree of lucidity, we will struggle. People buy results, so what result can you offer?

> 'Why should I buy from you?' There is plenty of competition out there

Most buyers, and this goes for consumers as well as professionals, will go through this kind of decision-making process before they buy anything:

- I'm OK: I have what I need.
- I am dissatisfied in some way – what I have is no longer OK.
- I decide to do something.
- I do some research – what are the options?
- I have some concerns – are these resolvable?
- I buy.
- I convince myself it was the right thing to do.

It's worth remembering this process as you go through the stages of a sale with a buyer. So let us focus on a practical application for you:

🡕 brilliant exercise

Take one of your key clients or prospects and put yourself in the buyer's shoes.

1 Go through this list of 20 questions and decide which of the questions above are likely to be on your buyers' minds.

2 What other questions might they have about your particular product / service?

3 As a buyer, attempt to answer the questions.

4 What fears does he / she have?

5 Finally – take your time to decide what actions you can take so that you build more trust and either sell for the first time or win more business.

There is a fair amount of consistency across regions as to what buyers are looking for from their salespeople. Of course, they want respect, a sensible level of support, and advice when it is appropriate. The table below outlines the nine key qualities that buyers are seeking from a sales partner, identified by DDI.

What are the top 3 qualities you value the most in a salesperson?

	Global	Australia	Canada	France	Germany	UK	US
Product or Service Advice	67%	70%	64%	72%	76%	58%	59%
Market Knowledge	44%	42%	44%	36%	58%	41%	41%
Trust	43%	47%	57%	40%	15%	49%	51%
Pricing/Price Negotiation	41%	47%	44%	35%	29%	49%	45%
Relationship Building	31%	34%	34%	24%	30%	33%	32%
Delivery Expediting	30%	23%	22%	40%	47%	26%	24%
Customer & Supplier Interface	24%	21%	22%	20%	36%	24%	23%
Business Advice	8%	5%	6%	15%	7%	6%	7%
ROI Analysis	4%	1%	2%	13%	1%	1%	4%

Take a careful look at the above table. Now, all salespeople are taught that people will only buy if there is a match between what someone is selling and what another wants or needs. So the above table is one of the most important parts of Brilliant Selling. This table represents what your buyers want.

⌐ brilliant exercise

Take some time over the following exercise – commit yourself to researching and getting clear where your strengths and possible weaknesses are.

Your job here is to complete the grid so that you have a good sense of where you are now in your own development. If you are a sales manager, get your sales team to complete the task.

For a complete picture, first of all do your own self-analysis.

Next ask your sales manager to complete the grid.

Finally, find at least one trusted customer and ask him / her to complete the grid. Score between 0 and 5 (0 = I never deliver, 1 = very occasionally deliver, 2 = quite often deliver, 3= often deliver, 4= deliver well, 5 = deliver excellently).

	YOUR SCORE	SALES MANAGER	TRUSTED CLIENT
PRODUCT OR SERVICE ADVICE			
Market knowledge			
Trust			
Pricing / Price negotiation			
Relationship building			
Delivery expediting			
Customer and supplier interface			
Business advice			
ROI analysis			

▶

What do you notice?

Where are the similarities? These will probably be your core strengths.

In what areas are your lower average scores? These are likely to be your weaknesses.

Finally, ask yourself this:

What can I do in the next three months that is not reliant on any external factors but my own effort, which will improve my weak areas? – then commit yourself to taking action right now.

↗ brilliant recap

We have covered quite a lot of ground here and so by now you should have a much greater sense of the identity of the modern buyer and what he wants. What buyers want to see in salespeople can perhaps best be summed up by one DDI respondent in France who said: 'Truth, sincerity, knowledge of product and understanding of my needs as a client.' Is this what you (and your team) deliver regularly right now?

Key elements uncovered in this chapter include:

- Research suggests that many buyers have a low opinion of salespeople.
- Only 6% rated the sales profession 'excellent'.
- Buyers want answers about your offering, the legitimacy of your business, how you stack up against the competition, your price vs. the value you offer, when to buy, and you as an individual. Their key question is: why should I buy from you?'
- The four qualities buyers most look for from salespeople are product knowledge, market knowledge, trust and a good price.

So now we know what buyers think of us as salespeople and what they want, how do we influence them to buy from us? We need to become really good at prospecting.

CHAPTER 17

Prospecting
with purpose

In some organisations a salesperson is not expected to do any prospecting at all – this is all done via the marketing or telesales departments. In most businesses, and certainly if you run your own business, prospecting is critical. And yet it is amazing how salespeople find excuses not to prospect. The root of this failure to focus on prospecting consistently could be:

> it is amazing how salespeople find excuses not to prospect

- Fear of rejection.
- Poor time management.
- Dislike of the process.
- Not confident about what to do and what to say.

Maybe you have another favourite?

'Where oil is first found is in the minds of men' – Wallace Pratt, US pioneer petroleum geologist

So let us accept it can be tough, uncomfortable and sometimes disheartening to prospect. This chapter gives you some key guidelines with which to work. These ideas are taken from modelling people who are successful at this element of the sales process – known in sales circles, somewhat archaically, as the hunters.

brilliant definition

In the broad sense, prospecting refers to exploration – you could be prospecting for valuable minerals and ores, such as gold, silver, or oil. In sales, prospecting is the search for potential customers.

 brilliant exercise

When you think of sales prospecting, what pops up in your mind?

What stops us focusing more time on prospecting and performing the task well?

Research suggests that there are two key things that will determine how successful you are at prospecting: attitude and action.

You need to develop a healthy and positive attitude to prospecting and you need to take positive action to support it. The truth of the matter is that if we do not prospect, we do not win new accounts and our sales can stagnate or fall sharply because there is one certainty in sales – however good we are, we WILL lose customers. It is just in the nature of business – companies fail, they merge or are acquired or your contact is replaced. Change happens.

There are many myths around sales prospecting so let us dispel some of these and then look at how to prospect with purpose.

Myth 1: Prospecting is the same thing as sales

It's not about selling at this stage – it is about discarding people and organisations who do not fit your criteria for doing business. You are looking for the 'gold', for organisations which qualify to get to the next stage. In most sales scenarios the key qualification questions are:

- Will my product or service solve a problem for them?
- Can they afford it?
- Are they willing to spend?

The job of prospecting is to find qualified leads; people that are able to buy your product / service. Only after this process is complete should the selling begin.

Myth 2: Prospecting is a numbers game

Old-school thinking suggests you need to contact hundreds of people. Not necessarily! We do a lot of work with law firms and there are thousands of law firms in the UK. Our best prospecting campaign (including advertising and email) was to only 60 firms and we got 14 strong leads. So, it is about quality, not quantity.

Myth 3: Prospecting is time-intensive

Done well, prospecting can just take a few minutes. Do not waste time on people unmotivated or unable to buy. You may decide to contact them again at a later stage, but avoid pressing for more contact or interest if there is none! Remember to focus on the 'gold'.

> Remember to focus on the 'gold'

If you prospected competently for two hours per week you would start seeing great results within a month.

Myth 4: Scripts simply do not work

Many salespeople prospect on the telephone or face to face without any script or basic framework. Scripting is essential for a successful prospecting campaign. It allows you to test what key benefits and qualifying questions work. Of course you need to personalise the script and make sure it sounds natural, but create one initially and change it as required, depending on what is working.

Myth 5: You need to 'close' them on the appointment

Many sales representatives focus too much time on getting the appointment and later wonder why so many prospects then cancel. People do not like to say no, so they say yes and then cancel later by email or just exit stage left at the agreed time of the appointment.

Another idea is to send them some information first and follow up later, or tell them something new or of value on the first call. Either of these tactics adds an extra stage, but is more likely to produce better qualified initial appointments.

So now we are done with the myths, how do we prospect successfully? Here is a process which works.

The prospecting process

1 Identify prospects

Your prospects may be blindingly obvious – if you are selling gym equipment it may well be worth contacting local sports centres. If you sell wine, off-licences may be a good bet. However, with many products and services the potential end user is not always crystal clear. So you may have to start by identifying your prospecting criteria. With whom do you want to do business? You will either be identifying a business or an individual. This table will help you build a profile of your intended prospect.

Business	Individual
What market?	What demographic?
What turnover?	What income?
What geographical area?	What geographical area?
What roles in business?	What job roles?
What specific businesses?	What pastimes?
Existing or new users?	What family?

Then go out there and find these businesses or individuals – you may well also be employing marketing tools to help you in this journey.

Once you have identified a prospect it is critical to do some research before first contact.

2 Plan and research your prospects

Let us assume you are working in business-to-business sales. In order to make a first favourable impression, you need to identify some of the following about any prospect:

- Culture.
- Obvious problems or challenges.
- Principal areas of business that would benefit from your product / service.
- Is the business growing, stagnating?
- Merging or restructuring?
- Cutting costs, laying off staff?
- What are the market trends?
- What factors will make your product / service a 'must have' rather than a 'nice to have'?

Distil your research into what you want to say about them when you speak on the telephone – focus on these questions:

- Can you help?
- How?
- Have you done this before?
- What value did you bring?
- Do you have a case study / testimonial to support this?
- What is their likely spend with you?
- Who is the right person to contact?

Identify a number of **Valid Business Reasons** for a call – these could include a restructuring initiative, a new purchase, redundancies, or a new opening.

 exercise

What Valid Business Reasons (VBRs) can you think of for a prospect wanting to talk to you?

Think about whether you really want them as customers:

- Does their profile match your ideal profile of a customer?
- What is their likely ability to meet your target price points?
- Will they have the ability to buy your minimum quantities?
- Who is the competition? What does this tell us?

You will then be in a position to contact them. Options that were identified by over 200 successful salespeople in our Brilliant Selling Survey (**www.brilliant-selling.com**) included:

- pitching up at a customer's premises
- sending samples
- an introductory email
- direct mail
- simply making a telephone call
- getting a referral from a customer or supplier
- using a telesales expert
- specific targeted campaigns
- hosting a seminar
- speaking at a conference
- PR
- trade shows
- networking events.

When you call a company you should call about them and their business, not you and your company.

3 Plan the initial telephone call

What are you going to say? Identify your call structure and ideally find time to rehearse what you are going to say.

Create a basic script. This will help you measure your success and, paradoxically, will free you up to focus on any response, because you already know what you are going to say.

Think about any objections you might meet – what are they likely to be and how would you handle them?

Possible objection	Ways of meeting objection

4 Get into a resourceful state

Your first call to a prospect could well be with a PA, or you might get lucky and make it direct to the prospect.

Ensure you are in a resourceful state to make the initial telephone call. This is key. (There is more information on this in Part 2 – influencing.)

For the purposes of this call, try some of these ideas:

- Say positive things to yourself – the prospect will like me / the company will benefit from my services / I want to find out more about them / The PA is a gate opener not a gate keeper.
- Stretch and feel physically relaxed.
- Stand up – you will feel better and more in control.
- Smile – it relaxes you and your voice.
- Use music – play a favourite energising tune.

- Take a stroll.

- Speak to someone you like.

5 Make the initial call to organisation

Your initial call structure with a PA or gatekeeper might look like this:

- Greet – your name, position and company.

- State your Valid Business Reason(s) for call.

- Check he / she is the right person.

- Request a brief telephone call when it is convenient, and book.

- Thank them.

Treat gatekeepers and PAs with immense respect. Explain to them the proposition as though they are the decision maker. It is surprising how many bosses trust the opinions of their PA. Treat them as a potential ally and not an obstacle. Treating them as an obstacle is a self-fulfilling prophecy.

Build rapport with whomever you speak. You can do this easily by remembering that it is not what you say but how you say it that will have

listen for what they say – and match language

the most impact. So, focus on how the person you are influencing speaks: the speed, volume and tone of the voice as well as how they breathe. Also, listen for what they say – and match their language. Remember that on the telephone we only have the voice and the words on which to focus.

6 Make the initial call to prospective buyer

All of the above is also relevant when you make the initial call to the prospect. Remember that here your key objective is to get an appointment with the prospect. Ideally call in the morning, and not on a Monday or Friday

Your call structure might look like this:

- Greet – your name, position, and company.
- State your valid business reason(s) for call – reiterate what worked with the initial call.
- Make link with PA or other person in their business.
- Identify what some of the key challenges are for the prospect.
- Use qualification questions to test level of interest.
- Define one key benefit for meeting with you, from the perspective of the prospect – use their language and include benefit statements so you make it compelling!
- Give one case study / testimonial to support above if required.
- Request a meeting – give a couple of alternatives and confirm time and date.
- Thank them.

7 Follow up all calls

Always follow up telephone conversations with emails confirming what was said and agreed. This will improve your credibility and will be good for people who like to reflect on conversations.

If the prospect has agreed to meet you then we have momentum and can focus on the first face-to-face meeting.

 brilliant recap

Certainly, prospecting can be tough at times, and yet there is the prospect of mining some real gold. If you have to prospect as part of your sales role you need to:

- Forget the myths of prospecting – they are just excuses for not taking action.
- Adopt a great attitude.
- Focus on the activity on a regular basis.
- Create and follow a tried and tested process, to follow which will ensure prospects become buyers as quickly as possible. It is likely to include these steps – identify your prospects, research them, plan your initial call, get into a resourceful state, make the calls and follow up.

Adopt these four ideas and you will get yourself some face-to-face meetings fairly rapidly!

CHAPTER 18

Initial meeting(s) with prospect

You have made the calls and got the appointment – now is your chance to find out what your prospect wants and start selling yourself as a problem solver and credible business partner.

Depending on your market, and your approach (transactional or consultative) there could be just the one meeting or several meetings before any decision is made about a purchase. It is possible your first meeting may even end up with an order. This is often the case with the FMCG (fast moving consumer goods) market.

If it is possible, include one other person (connected to the sale in some way) in this first (and, ideally, subsequent) meeting; '2-up' selling has some real benefits – it means it can be more interesting for the buyer, it relieves pressure, and it can be a more creative meeting. It is the old idea that two heads are better than one!

In this first meeting make sure you add some value in some way. Come armed with new information on their business or the market. In our Brilliant Selling Survey (**www.brilliant-selling.com**) 92% of successful salespeople who responded confirmed that they attempt to educate the customer on a regular basis.

*You don't get paid for the hour. You get paid for the **value** you bring to the hour.'* – Jim Rohn, US entrepreneur, author and motivational speaker

Think carefully about these two specific points before your next meeting with a prospective buyer:

1 Do more research

Buyers are bored with boring questions. They will either inwardly groan or outwardly yawn if you come up with questions like:

- So – how's business?
- Can you tell me about how you are organised?
- What's happening in the market?

You should know the answers to these situational questions! You can only do this if you do the research – use the internet, read the market journals, speak to people in your organisation, and come armed with facts. Buyers get turned off if they are asked questions that do not add value to their thinking.

Be prepared for all meetings and do some digging to find out what is happening in a business.

In a first meeting with a new prospect, these are the minimum things you may need to know:

- Facts and figures on turnover, margins and profitability.
- Organisational structure.
- History of the business.
- Recent important internal news – acquisitions, etc.
- Basic job overview of the buyer.

2 Be patient

One key issue we have seen with many of the sales forces with whom we have worked is that often salespeople give up too quickly . Would you buy first time from someone you had not met before? It once took me 12 months to convert an FMCG account but their first order was my biggest of the quarter! We recently won some business from a top 15 accountancy firm after 18 months and five meetings. The first order was for well over £17,000.

In case you have not been convinced yourself of this fact yet, allow us to share with you some statistics which should scare the living daylights out of salespeople:

48% of salespeople never follow up with a prospect

25% of salespeople make a second contact and stop

12% of salespeople only make three contacts and stop.

So – only 15% of salespeople make more than three contacts. What does this mean, then? Well, it means 85% of salespeople consistently waste golden opportunities to sell!

Because...

> only 15% of salespeople make more than three contacts

2% of sales are made on the first contact

3% of sales are made on the second contact

5% of sales are made on the third contact

10% of sales are made on the fourth contact

80% of sales are made on the fifth to twelfth contact.

So, if you are like almost half of all salespeople and make no more than one follow-up to your prospects, you are leaving 98% of your income on the table for someone else to come along and pick up.

> 80% of sales are made on the fifth to twelfth contact

recap

Here is a summary of what really matters in a first meeting:

● Always add value – in every meeting!

● If possible bring someone else in to your first meeting(s)

● Do the research – buyers are easily bored and often underwhelmed by salespeople!

● Be patient – it is not always possible to strike gold first time!

CHAPTER 19

Identifying what the prospect wants and needs

Whether you are involved in transactional or consultative selling it is imperative that you spend time identifying and agreeing what it is that your prospect and his organisation wants and needs. Avoid selling too quickly. People do not like being sold to. Do you? Usually we become defensive if we know someone is attempting to sell something. So – stop it! Build the relationship, develop trust, listen carefully and keep your overt selling to yourself!

'You will get all you want in life if you help enough other people get what they want.' – Zig Ziglar, author, salesperson and motivational speaker

At this stage you are looking to identify what the buyer needs and wants. What are the distinctions?

 brilliant definition

A **need** is something you have to have, something you cannot do without to survive.

A **want** is something you would like to have. It has emotional pull. And I cannot emphasise enough – a want pulls the emotional strings of desire.

Wants relate to emotions, whereas needs relate to something definitive within the specific business.

Generally, people buy what they want. They often don't buy what they need. It may be that what they want is what they think they need, but they could be very wrong about what they need. Beware! Prospects often do not know what they want. This may be because they do not know what is available. As Henry Ford suggested, 'If I had asked my customers what they wanted they'd have said a faster horse'! Buyers sometimes need educating in order that they want the right thing (which hopefully is your product / service).

Do you use a fabric conditioner in your house? Very few people were crying out for this product before it was launched by Unilever in the UK in 1969. Now, most modern washing machines have a dispenser which can add liquid fabric softener to the load of laundry automatically, and the market is worth £1 million per year.

Do you remember when an Iraqi journalist (Muntazar al-Zaidi) threw a shoe at George W Bush in December 2008? He was subsequently imprisoned. Ramazan Baydan, the owner of an Istanbul shoe company, was inundated with orders and had to recruit another 100 staff to cope with the demand. Many people buying probably did not need a new pair of shoes, but they certainly wanted one!

SPIN® selling

We can identify the needs and wants of prospects by asking questions and listening actively (for more on this see Part 3 – The power to influence). Specifically, when you are in the needs identification stage it is sensible to remember the SPIN® model for needs identification. British research psychologist Neil Rackham, whose company, Huthwaite Inc., has taught it to hundreds of corporations worldwide, developed the 'SPIN®' selling system. It involved 12 years of research and analysis of 35,000 sales situations.

At the heart of the system, explained in Rackham's book *SPIN Selling*, is a precisely defined sequence of four question types that enables the salesperson to move the conversation logically from exploring the customer's needs to designing solutions, or in Rackham's terms, to uncover Implied Needs and develop them into Explicit Needs that you, the salesperson, can resolve. SPIN® is the best researched sales methodology around and modelled on what Brilliant Salespeople do on a regular basis to identify what the prospect wants and needs. It is especially useful in complex or big ticket sales or if you use a consultative approach to selling.

The template can be used with both prospects and existing customers.

Here are the four types of questions identified by Rackham:

1 Situation questions

Every good seller begins the sales call by assessing the business terrain, by asking questions to clarify the customer's current situation. So Situation Questions are essential to gather information, but here is the surprise. Huthwaite's research found that, as valuable as they are, Situation Questions can be overused by inexperienced salespeople.

In big sales, minimise the small talk and focus on finding background detail that can be used to make sense of the buyer's business situation. This is about understanding the wider context of the prospect's business, before you zoom into the details.

Do not ask a question to elicit information that you could easily have obtained before beginning the call, during the research phase. And remember, when overused, these questions *bore* the customer.

Examples of situation questions:

'What's your position?'

'Who are your current suppliers?'

'Other than you, who are the key decision makers?'

'What is your vision for your business?'

 brilliant exercise

What sort of situation questions do you / could you ask?

2 Problem questions

Questions that are designed to identify a customer's problem are more often asked by experienced salespeople. The more experienced you become, the more you *want* to uncover difficulties. You start to understand that customer difficulties present you with an opportunity to be of service. One caveat, though: Huthwaite's research suggests that the effectiveness of these questions is inversely proportional to the size of the sale under consideration. They are most effective in smaller-ticket transactions.

> The more experienced you become, the more you *want* to uncover difficulties

A trap here is to dive straight into presenting the benefits of what you are selling. Going straight to the sales pitch will simply raise objections.

Examples of problem questions:

'What are the key challenges facing you in your business right now?'

'How satisfied are you with your current suppliers?'

'What kind of obstacles are you facing in this area?'

'How do these challenges manifest themselves?'

exercise

What sort of problem questions do you / could you ask?

3   Implication questions

These are questions about the 'effects, consequences or implications of the customer's problems'. They are strongly linked to success in larger-ticket sales and yet they are more difficult to phrase than either Situation Questions or Problem Questions. But they are essential to moving larger sales forward.

Instead of telling them the problem they have (which is also likely to raise objections), the goal is now to get them to see (and feel!) the problem. By being asked questions which draw out the implications of the problem, the buyer gets to feel the pain, that will drive them towards your product / service.

People are motivated by moving away from pain or towards pleasure (for more on this go to Part 1, You). These questions are intended to make the problem more acute for the buyer.

Examples of implication questions:

'What effect does this (problem) have?'

'What sort of risk would this constitute if nothing was done about it?'

'What does this reduction in income mean for growth?'

'What would happen if you did nothing?'

 exercise

What sort of implication questions do you / could you ask?

4   **Need-Payoff questions**

Need-Payoff questions are linked to success in more complex sales. They can be especially useful when you are talking to top decision makers (or those who will influence them), and they increase the likelihood that your solution, if accepted, will provide the payoff that answers the need. These questions focus the customer's attention on the solution rather than the problem, and they encourage him or her (with your assistance) to outline the benefits that your solution will provide his or her company. The focus is on the 'pleasure' of solving the problem. A good Need-Payoff question both pre-empts objections and enlists customer buy-in.

Examples of Need-Payoff questions:

'Is it important for you to solve the problem?'

'How do you think a faster supply chain solution would help you?'

'What kind of solution would best fit your current needs?'

'What sort of benefits would you see if something was done about this?'

 exercise

What sort of Need-Payoff questions do you / could you ask?

| The logic of the SPIN® process is common sense | The logic of the SPIN® process is common sense. The problem with common sense is that it is often not too common! |

As Rackham acknowledges, the SPIN® model is not a revolutionary discovery. Putting these four questions together in an orderly sequence, Rackham gives the following thumbnail definition of the SPIN® Selling model. It is simply 'the way most successful people sell on a good day when the call is going well.'

Make your prospect feel that you care. Make it easy for the customer to order. Do not focus on selling but identify the challenges and issues in the business and ask questions which turn up the heat and give the buyer an oppor-

> Do not focus on selling but identify the challenges and issues in the business

tunity to see there would be benefits to addressing the problem.

↗ brilliant recap

This final chapter in the section on buyers and prospects is pivotal. If you are unable to identify and agree what a buyer wants, you are in danger of becoming a desperate salesman who tries to position his product / service as a solution to all known problems. Here is a summary of what is covered in this chapter:

● There is a difference between wants and needs. Buyers buy what they want.

● We uncover what a buyer wants and needs through carefully structured questioning and active listening.

● The sequence for asking these questions is SPIN® (situation, problem, implication, need-payoff), which models the questions that successful salespeople ask.

PART 5

Presenting
solutions

I still remember my first day as a salesman. I was well prepared. I had undergone six weeks of rigorous training and I was pretty watertight on many of the key product lines. I had my new car, clean and polished. My case was full and neat. My shoes were shiny, my suit was pressed, and my shirt was ironed. I was a man on a mission – ready for action! And so I went to talk to buyers and prospects – lots of them. And I told them all about our fabulous product range. No-one bought from me on that first day even though I presented (I thought) wonderfully! After a week, only a handful had bought. I was worried. My area manager was due to come out with me. I was even more worried. Once he had spent a morning with me, his feedback was straight to the point – 'Your product knowledge is great – you know your stuff. But you are not relating it to the customers. Sell solutions, not products.' Good advice then, still good advice now.

So that is what this part is all about – presenting solutions to customers and prospects. You might be selling complex solutions, every day FMCG (fast moving consumer goods) deals, two-minute pitches on the telephone, or part of a procurement process that can takes weeks and endless bits of paper. Whatever your situation there will be areas of interest that will help you improve the way you deliver a solution to customers so it is compelling, persuasive and focused on them!

This section will focus on how to persuade with conviction and clarity. It will answer some important questions:

- How do we use benefit selling that does not sound contrived?
- How do you identify what to focus on when you sell?
- What should be included in a written proposal?
- How do you prepare effectively for a formal sales presentation?
- What does a persuasive delivery look like, sound like and feel like?
- How do you handle a genuine objection effectively?
- What has closing got to do with modern selling?

CHAPTER 20

Appealing to the customer

There has been a lot written about features and benefits in selling. The intention here is to cut through the fluff and focus on what really matters when it comes to positioning a product or service. Taking the time to communicate clearly the benefits to your target market will lead to a message that will resonate with your buyers, leading to increased sales of your product or service.

*'The future lies in designing and **selling** computers that people don't realize are computers at all'* – Adam Osbourne

Let us be clear about some distinctions immediately:

brilliant definition

A **Feature** is any characteristic of a product or service that remains the same whether the prospect or customer buys or not. These characteristics can include size, quality, payment terms, specialisation, technical details, factory location, product specifications (including size, weight, or colour) or anything else to do with describing the details of your product / service or company.

An **Advantage** is the performance characteristic of a service that describes how it can be used or will help the customer. Advantages are what some features provide. Examples of advantages are a

▶

photocopier that copies two sides of a page at once, or a coffee shop that offers wireless Internet access.

Benefits are the favourable results that the buyer receives from the service / product because of a particular advantage that has the ability to satisfy a customer's need / want. Benefits are statements which explicitly demonstrate how your service / product meets the needs of a customer. A benefit describes the individual value the advantage has for this particular customer as defined by his / her unique goals and priorities.

USP: Unique selling proposition – something you or your company has that no other company has.

Key differentiator: A feature that is better than the main competitor in some way(s).

brilliant example 1

Feature: Power steering

Advantage: Fluid is pumped into a cylinder that helps make the wheels turn with less effort.

Benefit: Makes parking easier – reduces the time it takes to get into a tight space.

brilliant example 2

Feature: Wrist watch

Advantage: Tells you the time accurately

Benefit: Ensures you are not late to important appointments.

Think about it – what is important here is the benefit, not the advantage or feature. Too often, we promote features when it is benefits that our customers are buying. We buy petrol to go places not because of the value of the liquid itself. Nobody who bought a drill wanted a drill. They wanted a hole. Here's a revelation: skydivers don't need parachutes. What they need is what the parachute does for them. Specifically, they need a tool to slow themselves down before they hit the ground. If there were a better way to soften the impact than a parachute, the parachute's days might be numbered. Think about what has happened to the typewriter, or the slide rule.

Although we sometimes seem to get attached to certain products it is, after all, the benefits of the product that we seek. Not, generally, the features or the advantages.

In sales, we do well to realise that people buy benefits, not features or advantages. Whether you are in B2B sales, B2C sales, internet sales, retail sales, or you are selling professional services, benefits are what sell your product or service. The trick is to orientate our presentations and sales conversations, either face to face or on the telephone, so that we present **selective** benefits – not features – to the customer. Because buyers are now more sophisticated they will get turned off by poor use of the feature–benefit model, which was born out of the transactional method of selling.

> people buy benefits, not features or advantages

You can help yourself to differentiate between features and benefits as you develop sales presentations, by stating a feature and then linking that with a benefit with 'which means' and / or 'so that'. For example: Power steering helps make the wheels turn with less effort **which means that** it makes parking easier and reduces the time it takes to get into a tight space.

The focus of your communication should be on how your product / service can solve, address, improve, or reduce any area of difficulty that the specific customer / prospect outlines. When we consider the benefits we will be articulating to the buyer, it will be helpful to ask these sorts of questions:

- How will my product or service solve a problem for the customer?
- How will my service fulfill a client's want / need?
- In what way is my product better than the competition's?
- How does my price compare?
- Will my service improve the customer's life? Make her happier? Reduce risk? Make her more productive? Reduce costs in the long run?
- Does my product last longer than the competition's?

The key point here can be positioned in one sentence:

'Most buyers will buy because of the benefits to them of your product / service (and because a problem is being solved), not the specific features that are part of the product / service.'

If you really think about it, you can link most benefits at the highest level to:

1 Money: The product or service helps the buyer make or save money and so improves competitiveness.

2 Time: The product or service helps the buyer save time or frees up time for doing other things and so increases efficiency.

3 Ego: The product or service in some way makes the buyer feel good or increases work / life balance.

Make all benefits customer-focused

But forget about selling generic benefits. The knack in representing benefits is to focus on the specific problems and issues of the customer in front of you. Make all benefits customer-focused.

You will lack credibility if you focus just on generic benefits. Specific benefits must be supported by features. A benefit statement such as, 'Our new software will improve productivity by as much as 20%, saving you £29,000 per year and paying for itself within fourteen months' must be accompanied by the features that bring about those benefits, or your target market won't believe the benefits – they will have no credibility.

Many salespeople fall into the trap of spending too much time on selling features. I wanted to buy a flat screen TV just after Christmas. I went into a high street shop and the salesperson started talking to me about pixels, colour decoding infrared commands, and compatible HDMI devices. What was important to me was that it went on the wall nicely, that the picture quality was good and that it would be child friendly. I was not asked what I wanted, however. I had to stop him after a few minutes and tell him!

So he got a second chance and I did buy a TV, but you may not get a second chance to present a solution, so you need to know the most effective ways of delivering persuasive information. Buyers always buy to move away from problems or something that creates pain (in this case, the large space that my TV took up in the lounge) and / or towards pleasure (in this case much improved picture and HD ready). They always buy to solve specific problems.

I have seen business experts from major organisations include these sorts of things in sales presentations:

- When the business was established.
- How many offices they have.
- Multiple service offerings.
- Organisation of the sales force.

None of these are particularly relevant unless they are linked with the buyer's interests / problems.

Most products or services have many features that could be attractive to a buyer. The trick is to align what you say with the interests of the prospect / buyer. The importance of benefits will change, dependent on the target audience. In many cases, a variety of decision makers (and influencers) are involved in a purchasing decision. You must tailor your promotional materials and your sales presentation to each one.

> align what you say with the interests of the prospect / buyer

In many sales situations you know who you are competing against. One step to take before deciding your sales focus is to identify what areas are likely to be of most interest to the buyer. You can do this by completing this table:

USPs vs. the competitor	Key differentiators	Same as	Worse than

Basically you will be focusing your sales efforts in the 'USPs' (if you can think of any) and the 'key differentiators'. The reality is that because of fierce competition it may be that you can find no 'USPs' – so you need to focus on your 'key differentiators', from the point of view of the customer.

The 'same as' and 'worse than' features are likely to be some of the objections you may face.

exercise

So go ahead and do try this out.

Step 1: Specifically identify a customer group to which you want to communicate

Step 2: Describe your product or service in 25 words or less.

Step 3: List the problems your product or service solves for the above customer group and / or the needs and wants the product or service meets for the group.

Step 4: With the above information in mind, complete the table below.

Step 5: Test each feature and benefit statement using the 'So what?' test. One of the difficulties in crafting our own feature and benefit statements is that the benefits of a particular feature are so clear to us that we assume they are evident to our target market as well. A dangerous assumption! If it is really not persuasive then eliminate it from the sales presentation.

You will now have the basics of how to position your product or service.

Compared to the competition, here is how I stack up:

USPs vs. the competitor	Key differentiators	Same as	Worse than

↗ brilliant recap

This chapter has been about how we position what we want to sell. So here, in summary, are the key points to remember:

● Many buyers are just not interested in features in isolation.

● There is a distinction between features, advantages, and benefits and Brilliant salespeople know how and in what sequence to articulate the distinctions.

● Buyers buy benefits which solve specific problems.

● Choose benefits that differentiate your product or service from the competition – if you have real USPs then tell buyers!

CHAPTER 21

Writing great sales proposals

Winning business in today's highly competitive market often means you will have to write some type of proposal. Whether you are trying to win a new customer or sell an idea to a current customer, your sales proposal is unlikely to win you the deal, but it could easily lose you the deal.

'Few writers think of the messages they are trying to communicate in a report.' – Bruce Ross-Larson, Riveting Reports

Your proposal is a sales, not a technical, document. It is imperative that you demonstrate your credibility, understanding, and customer focus in every proposal that you present to your

> demonstrate your credibility, understanding, and customer focus in every proposal

customer or prospect. What can you do to produce a high-quality sales document that gets results? Just follow these ten commandments to get you to the promised land!:

1 Elicit criteria for the proposal

When you are with your prospect / buyer, and you have got
to the point when it has been agreed that you should write a
proposal, spend some time identifying what the decision
maker would like to see in the proposal. Avoid assumptions.
Simply ask questions like:

- What would you like to see in this proposal?
- What will a really good proposal look like for you?
- What annoys you in proposals?
- Who is going to be reading this document?
- Are you a big picture or detail person?

Once you have elicited the criteria, summarise and then
confirm this by email. You are getting lots of yes's before
anything has been written and demonstrating that you are
customer focused.

2 **Under-promise and over-deliver**

Think carefully before you commit to getting the proposal back to the buyer by a certain date. Most proposals do not have to be written yesterday, however pressing the requirement. You know how annoying it is when you are on a train that has stopped and the conductor informs you that you will be leaving in just a few minutes. If you are stuck there twenty minutes later it feels even worse – so avoid this trap. It is best to pick a date that is realistic and then complete it ahead of time. In this way you are under-promising and over-delivering. Customers love this.

3 **Make sure proposals are customer focused**

When you start writing the proposal, ensure that you focus on the customer. Customers need to know that they have been heard and understood. Customers expect you to be responsive to the requirements that they have outlined, whether those requirements were provided verbally or documented in a formal request for proposal (RFP). If the prospective client has sent you an RFP, read it assiduously. Most RFPs include specific guidelines regarding submitting your sales proposal – so, do what you are told!

Use their language – identify their concerns, and their challenges. Focus on matching any proposal with a need or want that has been identified in the needs analysis selling phase. Cite your customer's name throughout the proposal. I always note specific words down when I am making notes during an initial meeting – and then play these hot buttons back to the buyer in the proposal. It demonstrates that you were listening and that you can empathise!

4 **Brainstorm**

Whether you write the proposal in isolation or as part of a team, spend some time brainstorming. Identify lots of things you could include and then start paring it down to a

manageable chunk of information. Here are the sorts of
questions that will get your creative juices flowing:

- What is the customer's core issue?
- Why is this problem so important?
- What does the customer want?
- What are the measurement criteria?
- What options does the customer have?
- What is our value proposition?
- How can we prove that it will work?

Once the brainstorming is over you can start outlining your
proposal and preparing a rough draft.

5 **Use a template**

Create a basic template that you can adapt for each
proposal. It will save you time. A typical proposal will
include:

- Executive summary.
- Introduction.
- Identification of issues / challenges.
- Alternatives.
- Recommendation.
- Process – show the steps to provide whatever it is your
  potential client needs.
- Cost of investment.
- Summary.

For more information about proposal templates see
www.brilliant-selling.com.

6 **Write well**

We all have different styles, but here are some basics to bear
in mind. Use these guidelines to make your proposal easy to
read and evaluate:

- Use section headings to help the reader understand the logic
  of your proposal.

- Avoid confusing sentence structures – keep sentences short and coherent.

- Avoid using words, expressions or three-letter acronyms that will not be readily understood by the reader.

- Use 10-12 point font size.

- Limit paragraph length. Lengthy paragraphs appear text-heavy, so restrict your paragraphs to 10 lines.

- Break up the text with some visuals and graphics. Effective proposal graphics can include charts, photographs, cartoons, graphs, and diagrams.

7 **Substantiate all claims you make in your proposal**

Buyers will be on the lookout for over-exaggerated claims. Ensure you can back up what you are saying. Use real-life examples, case studies and illustrate how your organisation differs from and is better than the competition.

> Buyers will be on the lookout for over-exaggerated claims

8 **Offer alternatives**

We often position our proposals as discussion documents. Proposals can often seem too formal and restrictive. Identify a number of alternatives and your buyer will then feel as though she has more choice. Your proposal should, ideally, include all alternatives – including what the competition is or may be offering and the consequences of doing nothing. Too often proposals are done too quickly and are too limited in scope. Ensure there is room for creativity and input from the customer.

9 **Write a strong Executive Summary**

An Executive Summary is often the last thing you write but the first thing that the customer reads. It provides a consolidated summary of all the key points that are included in your proposal.

Let us be realistic. Many buyers, and especially others involved in the decision-making process, will simply choose not to read your entire document. So ensure your Executive Summary is accurate, interesting and persuasive – avoid grovelling or profusely thanking the buyer for the opportunity. Customers should never have to search for your key responses.

10 Follow up and present if you can

Ideally you want to present the proposal at the same time as you deliver it. This may not always be practical. If you are unable to present formally, send a hard and soft copy of your proposal, and make sure it looks great. Telephone soon afterwards for feedback.

If you are able to present aspects of the proposal formally your chances of winning the work are immediately strengthened because you can answer queries and back up your recommended solutions with additional information.

 brilliant recap

Your sales proposal will not win you the deal but it could lose you the deal. It is more likely to win you the deal if you remember the ten commandments of great proposal writing:

- Elicit criteria.
- Under-promise and over-deliver.
- Make sure proposals are customer focused.
- Brainstorm.
- Use a template.
- Write well.
- Substantiate all claims you make in your proposal.
- Offer alternatives.
- Write a strong executive summary.
- Follow up and present.

If you are able to present, the next section will provide you with some ideas about how to make a real impact when making sales presentations.

CHAPTER 22

Preparing winning pitches

*S*ales presentations can come in many different guises. Here are some contrasting ways in which people pitch for business:

- Formal or informal.
- Individual or as a team.
- In front of one / a few people or in front of many people.
- Long or short.
- With questions or without questions.
- With visual aids or without visual aids.

How do you present now? There are many great books out about presenting so I want to focus specifically on sales presentations. Whatever way you and your company present, this is where you really earn your money. This is the performance element – get this wrong and you can be out of the door swiftly. Get it right and your presentation can be the differentiator that wins you the business. As with so many aspects of sales, it all starts with the preparation ...

How to write a great sales presentation for a formal pitch

'Men stumble upon the truth from time to time, but most pick themselves up and hurry off as if nothing has happened.' – Winston Churchill

This section is aimed at salespeople who have to deliver a formal pitch, perhaps on the back of a proposal. There is a six-step process to effective preparation for a sales presentation. So let us look at each step in some detail.

1   Identify your outcome

identify the reason why you are speaking

Your first step in preparation is to identify the reason why you are speaking; what you hope to achieve. Do this by visualising an ideal outcome. How do you want your audience to feel, to think, and what do you want them to do as a result of your presentation?

Identify the positive audience reaction that you want, e.g. 'By the end of my presentation we want them to have confidence in my new proposals and be eager to start implementing them.'

What do you want them to take away from your presentation? If there is one core message, what is it?

2   Research your audience

find out as much as possible about your audience

You need to find out as much as possible about your audience before you begin your preparation. For example:

- Why are they there? What are they expecting? What are their wants and needs?
- How much do they know about the subject?
- How much do they need to know so that you will achieve your objective?
- What is their attitude likely to be to you and your organisation?
- Have they any past experience that will influence them towards or against you?

- Are decision makers present?
- Will they read your proposal beforehand?

You need to plan your whole presentation from the point of view of your audience. Only include material that will be of interest, benefit or concern to them. Use examples that they can relate to. Ask yourself, 'If I were in their shoes, what would I want to hear?'

> 'If I were in their shoes, what would I want to hear?'

Researching your audience will also enable you to establish a rapport with them at the start of your sales presentation by showing that you understand their problems and concerns.

brilliant tip

Wherever possible and when appropriate always try to contact the individuals you will be presenting to in advance. This enables you to build some rapport before you present to them.

The key point here is that all sales presentations should be audience-centric rather than you-centric.

3   Brainstorm

You may or may not be part of the creative element of putting a presentation together. There may be a temptation to 'cobble' a sales presentation together using previous presentations and only making small adjustments. Avoid this mistake!

If you are part of the team, or if you are producing a presentation yourself, you can't be creative and organised at the same time – ideas don't come in order, so use an Ideas Map to brainstorm your topic as follows:

- Write the subject of your presentation in a circle in the centre of a large sheet of paper.

- Write down all the ideas and thoughts you have on the subject, starting from the circle and branching out along lines of connecting ideas. Ideally use different coloured pens.

- Let your mind be as free as possible. Do not restrict your thoughts by deciding where each point should go in a list. Your ideas show flow easily.

- When you have finished, link any related ideas and sections.

  Now you are ready to select the appropriate information to include in your presentation.

4 **Select and structure your material**

When you have completed your Ideas Map, you will almost certainly have more material than you require to deliver a great sales presentation. Now start selecting suitable information against your specific objective, your audience's needs and expectations and the time available. Avoid going straight to creating a slideshow.

A mistake in a pitch is to think you have to tell them everything about you and your organisation. Audiences are generally interested in what you can do for them! So go for a simple structure that focuses on the audience's interests.

Nobody can remember a great mass of detail – and they almost certainly don't need to, either. If you give people too many facts you overload them, and they end up remembering nothing. So, concentrate on a few key facts. Ask yourself 'If my audience goes away remembering only three or four key facts, which ones should they be? What is critical for them to know so that they can make a judgment about our suitability?'

You need to find examples and anecdotes to illustrate your key facts and bring your presentation alive. Many presentations fail because they are over-dependent on facts and lack imaginative word pictures.

Your presentation must have a logical structure. There are many possibilities – for example, a chronological sequence, or points in the order of importance, or showing the problem followed by the solution, or an explanation of theory followed by a demonstration of how it works in practice. Select the best structure for your objective and audience. It will help you if you give each section and sub-section a clear and specific heading. We tend to use a formula created by Bernice McCarthy in the US in the 1970s. The idea is that you break your presentation into specific sections, each one reflecting different preferences that will be there in the audience – **WHY?, WHAT?, HOW?, WHAT IF?**

- **WHY** is this important to the audience? – get them motivated to listen. Cover the why at the beginning of your sales presentation.

- **WHAT** – the audience needs information.

- **HOW** – is it going to work? You might demonstrate how a system or product works or the process that follows a purchase.

- **WHAT IF** – for those who wish to explore the future consequences of buying your product / service. What sort of impact is it going to have on the business?

The 4-mat system is practical, easy to understand and easy to utilise in sales presentations.

Only start thinking about your visual aids when you know what you are going to say; don't plan your presentation round them.

5 Focus on the start and the finish

The start and finish of a presentation is critical, because of the primacy and recency effect – people tend to remember more easily what they witnessed first and last.

The start must be punchy, attention-getting and capture the audience immediately. It tells people why they should listen, what you are going to talk about and the scope of your presentation.

Here is what you need to cover:

- An introduction to you (if some or all in the audience do not know you).
- The length of time the presentation will last.
- When you intend to take questions.

brilliant tip

Finally, ensure you remember the COMB:

C = Context – relevance to the audience

O = Objective – the goal of the presentation

M = Map – the agenda that you will follow

B = Benefits – that is, the WHY – what's in it for them? What will they get as a result of listening carefully?

The conclusion should be short, definite and conclusive. Summarise the main points and, if appropriate, state the next action.

6 Practise

Always rehearse a sales presentation. Stand up, and do it for real. Do not keep going back to the beginning each time you stop – otherwise you may never rehearse the ending! Remember to time the whole talk, and aim to finish it a few minutes short of your time slot. Practise as a team, if appropriate, or in front of colleagues, and when possible, practise in the same room in which you are delivering the presentation.

🗲 brilliant recap

This six-step process is ideal as a process to follow when you are delivering a formal pitch. It will allow your sales presentation to be focused, creative and centred on the audience.

1 Identify your outcome.

2 Research your audience.

3 Brainstorm.

4 Select and structure your material.

5 Focus on the start and the finish.

6 Practise.

Once you have practised and made changes as appropriate, then you are ready to deliver the sales presentation. For a more detailed list of what to do before any sales presentation, please visit **www.brilliant-selling.com**.

CHAPTER 23

Persuasive delivery

We have all been subjected to boring or feature-heavy sales presentations, either face to face or on the telephone. They put us off buying. The key to a formal sales presentation is to really engage the audience – bored buyers do not buy. If

> bored buyers do not buy

you engage them, you stand a chance! In order to really engage any audience when you are delivering a formal sales pitch there are four areas that, if done well, will put you in the pantheon of great presenters:

- Strong and open body language.
- Visual aids that help the audience.
- Presenters that look like a team.
- Presentations that hook the audience.

'To convert somebody go and take them by the hand and guide them.'
– Aquinas, St Thomas

Body language

Strong and open body language will support the content of any sales presentation. Here is how you do it:

- Get grounded by ensuring your feet are shoulder width apart and facing the audience. Stand tall and you will be perceived as a confident person. Undirected movement of the legs and feet shows that you are nervous and feel uncomfortable in front of the audience. Swaying, rocking, standing on one foot, and even little dances all reveal your inner anxiety. Learn to stand still and direct your energy to your audience.

- Allow your hands to fall to the side or clasped gently over your stomach. This is the most neutral resting position.

- Retain eye contact with the audience throughout, not like a scared rabbit that has to check all the escape routes, but in a calm and interested manner as you would when talking to a good friend. Avoid looking at:

  - Visual aids.

  - The floor or ceiling.

  - Your notes.

  - The most senior person present.

  - The friendliest person present.

  - Or even out of the window.

- In a formal sales presentation, always stand, if possible, as it will give you more authority, more breath and therefore a stronger voice, but above all it will give you the flexibility to move around and stay in control.

  Avoid the following:

  - Fiddling with rings, watches, cuff links, paper clips, glasses, coins in pockets or elastic bands.

  - Touching and patting hair, face, pockets, desk or table.

- Your gestures should coincide with what you are saying and naturally add emphasis to your words. Remember that gestures should include the whole of your arm and not be restricted to small, meaningless hand movements.

- Smile. It will make the audience want to listen to you instead of being discouraged by a hostile glare.

Ensure your visual aids are visual and aid the audience!

Avoid a slow death from a thousand slides. Too many people use too many slides during a presentation and basically bore the pants off people!

Many visual aids fail because they are not visual. They should be used to help the audience, and not as a prompt for the speaker. If you think part of your presentation may be boring without visual aids, work on making the **content** more interesting.

There are many visual aids available to you – story boards, products, posters, white boards as well as PowerPoint. Be creative, especially in pitches for new business. Here is a real chance to be distinctive and show why you are the best choice!

All visual aids should be simple, clear and visual. Their purpose is to help the audience, not to remind you of what you want to say.

> All visual aids should be simple, clear and visual

Good visual aids can:

- Show the relationship or comparison between data (bar chart or pie chart).
- Build up a picture.
- Show a process.
- Summarise key points.

Successful visual aids have:

- Bold contrasting colour.
- Consistency – the same background colour throughout and a uniform typeface.
- Simplicity – one idea per slide.
- Good design – so the eye moves to the essential elements.

What to avoid when designing visual aids:

- Reproduction of computer printouts.
- Tables of figures.
- Complex diagrams.
- Reproduction of forms.
- Excessive words (maximum of 7 words per line and 5 lines if using bullet points).

Before your presentation:

- Think carefully about where you are going to stand – don't block the screen.
- Make sure you know how to operate the equipment.
- Have all your visual aids in order, numbered clearly.
- Take a backup copy on a memory stick.

During your presentation:

- Do not show the visual aids until you are ready to talk about them.
- Introduce the whole visual before you start to talk about the detail.
- Give people time to look at them – don't whisk them off at top speed.
- Avoid talking to the visual aids. Remember, there are *people* out there who want to hear you!

Delivering sales presentations as a team

You may choose to present in teams when winning new business or retaining existing business. There are specific areas to focus on when you are presenting as a team, which are fundamental to

the success of the presentation.
There are sound reasons why a
team approach can work well.

> There are sound
> reasons why a team
> approach can
> work well

When we work with salespeople
who present in teams and have
been unsuccessful in winning a piece of business there are some
common themes that emerge from the feedback they receive
from customers:

- 'They presented more as a group of individuals rather than a single cohesive team.'

- 'They seemed uncertain as to who had responsibility for each section of the presentation.'

- 'They were not consistent in how they presented or in the quality of the presentation.'

Often, the team that presents to win some business does not
operate each day as a team so there is likely to be some lack of
familiarity between individuals. For a team presentation to be
effective, you must practise together and pay attention to how
you work as a team.

Here are some important tips on presenting as part of a team:

- Decide the key goal of the presentation and make sure that everyone presenting understands it.

- As you are planning your presentation make sure that you keep everyone in the loop in terms of amendments, changes in attendees or timings, etc. Make sure that no one is 'surprised' by anything on the day.

- Decide on who should be present based on what the customer / prospect needs. Everyone in the presenting team should add value.

- Make sure that everyone understands their specific role in the presentation. This is especially true if you are asking someone senior to present as part of your team.

- Make sure that you play to your strengths. Not everyone needs to present. It may be, for example, that you have a 'technical expert' there for questions even if they are not formally presenting.
- Make sure you rehearse together as a team. As part of rehearsing, it is important to:
  - Give each other specific, objective feedback on what they do well and what could be improved.
  - Rehearse the whole presentation from start to finish.
  - Agree and rehearse the handovers from one person to another (this is one area where a team can come across as uncoordinated!).
  - Agree on who will handle questions, and practise taking and answering some of the more challenging potential questions.
- During the presentation, support each other with positive body language: good eye contact, nodding, etc.

 tip

Email us at **resources@brilliant-selling.com** for a checklist relating to preparing for team presentations.

Final tips on how to engage the audience

'They may forget what you said, but they will never forget how you made them feel.' – Carl W. Buechner

The key thing with delivering a sales presentation is to engage the audience. Then they will really feel part of the presentation. Here are some final tips on how to do this:

- Get into a resourceful, confident state. To find out how to do this, take a look at Part 3 – The Power to Influence.

- Use sales materials wisely and sparingly. Used well, these will give your presentation more credibility and will probably be used during the HOW stage.

- Use multiple senses. Your audience will get distracted (however outstanding you are as a presenter). You need to find ways of getting them interested and holding their attention. One way of doing this is to engage as many senses as possible in a presentation. We see, hear, feel (external touch and internal emotion), taste and smell. Include as many of these senses as possible in your presentation. Here are some other suggestions:

- Have music playing – especially at the beginning and end of your presentation. It will engage the audience and help get them or keep them in the desired state.

- Ensure that there is visual stimulation. You may well be using a software package such as PowerPoint, but also consider:
  - Playing a video.
  - Putting banners / posters up around the room.
  - Using a flipchart.
  - Drawing a picture.

- Get your audience to do something, perhaps introduce themselves, explain their goals or answer a question. Involve them as much as you can.

- Most people at your presentations are interested in what you have to say, so words are important. You want to ensure that your words are working for you, and not getting lost. Use language, which covers the three main senses – **Visual**, **Auditory** and **Kinesthetic**:
  - **Visual**. See, look, picture, outlook, insight, reflect, glimpse, snapshot, brilliant, bright, colourful, illuminating

- **Auditory**. Hear, listen, sound, say, tune in, dialogue, ring, chime, quiet, tell, echo, announce

- **Kinesthetic**. Feel, grab, pull, grasp, get hold of, handle, tough, sharp, dig, impact

● Use your voice effectively: Make sure that you vary your voice tone so that it is interesting to your audience and makes them want to listen. Some presenters we have heard have quite monotone voices that do not, necessarily, inspire interest. Be aware of your volume and speed of delivery (you may need to slow down, for example). See Part 3 for more information about delivering with rapport and credibility.

⤴ ❭brilliant recap

In all formal buying situations that we have come across part of the selection criteria is how you present your product / service. We have seen it make and break a deal and it is an area in which you can really engage your audience with a passionate presentation which reinforces what you have to offer. The four presentation elements we have focused on in this chapter are:

● Strong and open body language (get grounded, have a resting position, retain eye contact, stand, use supportive gestures and smile).

● Visual aids that help the audience (ensure they are audience friendly, be creative, design them carefully, use them with a light touch).

● Presenters that look like a team (have goals, roles and support each other).

● Presentations that hook the audience (use sales materials wisely, use multiple senses, get your audience involved).

Even with the best sales presentations, there are likely to be objections that crop up. These need to be respected and handled well.

CHAPTER 24

Making the most of objections

In traditional sales training, sales people are often taught to 'overcome' an objection. If you were buying, would you really like your objection 'overcome'? You would surely feel more comfortable if any objection was handled sensitively and addressed sensibly.

An objection is a reservation, or concern, about some aspect of a service / product that may prevent a sale taking place. The old adage here is correct – objections can be buying signals. They suggest that there is interest. Stony silence or a definite 'no' indicates you have less chance of completing the sale! Objections may just be the buyer suggesting:

- 'Give me more information before I decide.'
- 'I need a little more proof that your product really will fill my needs.'
- 'I'm almost convinced, but I need just one more reason to justify me saying yes.'

Your task is to understand the reason for the concern and help provide a response that meets the concern.

'Nothing will ever be attempted if all possible objections must first be overcome.' – Samuel Johnson

What sort of objections do your buyers voice? Think about this question and list the most common objections that you encounter.

Typical objections involve:

- Price.
- Resistance to move to a new supplier (resistance to change is often a key motivator for objections).
- Concerns about some aspect of the product / service.
- Support offered.
- Timing (as in 'Let me think about it.').

Begin with the right attitude. A salesperson must never appear nervous or hesitant when an objection is raised. Hesitating or diverting the eyes loses trust. To remain calm, remember that objections are opportunities to learn more about the client's needs. Top salespeople understand this and are eager to discuss whatever issue a client raises.

> objections are opportunities to learn more about the client's needs

Often the best way to handle objections is to get them on the table at the beginning of your presentation or address them directly in your proposal. As in:

'I would imagine there are certain areas in which it would be important for you to gain some clarity ... I will directly address these during my presentation.'

Whatever the reason for an objection, the customer is, in effect, saying...

I am not yet totally convinced that your solution addresses my needs ... I am not sure I see the value or the benefit.

So here is a four-step process for handling objections successfully. It is known as the 4A model:

Acknowledge

Audience

Answer

Ask

- **A**cknowledge – the person who has made the objection – 'thanks for raising this – I can understand why this is an important area for you.'

- **A**udience – throw open, if appropriate, to the audience if there is more than one person. Ask some questions to get clarity and give you a bit of time to think:

  'On a scale of 1-10 how important is this?'

  'Does everyone else share this concern?'

If there is life without your product or service, then there is life with your product or service. The prospect will experience one of these two scenarios ... guaranteed. The question is, do they see enough difference between them to make a choice that is different from the status quo? So one way of handling an objection is to be very upfront and paint a picture of what it will be like both with and without your product / service. Just ensure that life with your product / service looks a lot rosier!

The only person who can really 'deal' with an objection is the buyer / prospect. Until the prospect handles the objection in her own mind, it is not handled. So what does the prospect need to go inside themselves and handle the objection in a way that allows the sale to proceed? Saying 'Trust me, I'm a saleswoman' is unlikely to work unless there is an extraordinary level of trust already built. So what information does the prospect need in order for HER to handle HER objection? Think of objection handling as facilitating a process within the prospect rather than directing a process at the customer.

> Think of objection handling as facilitating a process within the prospect

brilliant exercise

Take the objections you identified in the last exercise and identify what questions you can ask a buyer to facilitate his thinking:

Typical objection	Questions to ask

- Answer – now you have to address the issue. Avoid waffling, focus on making no more than three points, and keep it simple and directly address the problem. Avoid becoming defensive by trotting out features – answer the objection by linking to the customer's needs and selling value.

- Ask – the person who raised the objection if it has now been answered satisfactorily:

'How does that sound?'

'Has that addressed your concern?'

'Is there anything else you need to feel comfortable now?'

If the customer still has the concern then simply start at the first 'A' again and cycle through the process. It is sometimes possible, after you have completed the 4As process, to get commitment to buy the product / service there and then.

A common objection is often over price. This could in fact be a negotiation point. When faced with price concerns, probe:

- Before we talk about price, what other questions do you have about (insert your product / service)?
- What is your main concern about price?
- What do you need to know so that price is no longer an issue?

Then sell the value of your product / service before addressing the price concern.

Here are ten final tips about handling objections:

1   Audience profiling should have helped you to anticipate objections and identify potential sources of difficulty in your 'pitch'.

2   Prepare for objections as thoroughly as for the main sales presentation.

3   Anticipate the three to five objections that you really **do not** want to be asked – especially for competitive pitches, and ensure you know how to handle them well.

4   Prepare support materials in anticipation of likely objections.

5   Get feedback during a sales pitch as in – 'So, what do you think?' This will flush out some objections and avoid you getting a bunch of objections right at the end.

6   If you do not understand an objection ask for clarity.

7   Avoid arguing with a buyer – listen carefully and respond with empathy and logic.

8   Listen not only to the words and their meaning but also to whatever emotional content is expressed in the objection.

9   If the questioner rambles and is unclear, summarise the objection to help the audience understand what point you are now addressing.

10   If you are presenting as part of a team, decide who is going to handle which objections. To ensure cohesion you may choose to filter all objections through the leader of your team.

brilliant recap

Objections are likely to crop up in one form or another during a sale, and that's when you start earning your crust! The key points we want you to leave with are:

- Objections are often just buying signals in disguise.
- Anticipate objections and prepare how to answer them.
- Flush out any likely objections early.
- Avoid getting into a knockabout argument.
- Remain calm.
- Probe for more information.
- Answer the objection in a straightforward manner.
- Get agreement that the issue is sorted.

Objections do not have to be the stumbling blocks that they seem. Very quickly you can move towards commitment.

CHAPTER 25

Closing and commitment

still have the sales brochure for the first sales training I attended. The front cover proclaimed:

> # CLOSE
> # THAT
> # SALE

When I got to the location for the training, there were large posters with the same message, and underneath, '101 ways to get the buyer to say yes'. Wow! I was lost on about the 17th!

Up until the end of the 1980s there was a huge emphasis on closing as the magical, possibly mystical, element of selling. You will still find an enormous amount of material on the web which will show how to close. Maybe you do have to get lots of people to say yes regularly: certainly any salesperson knows that there may be a point when he asks for the business. However, in this book, this section will be one of the shortest. Why? Because people do not like to be 'closed'. Consumers, let alone professional buyers, are so much more savvy to 'closing techniques' and see them for the absurd attempts at manipulation that they are. We speak to many professional buyers and they lose respect for people who try to close before they are ready to buy.

Yes, of course customers still have to say 'yes', otherwise we would all be out of a job. But, no, buyers hate salespeople who use tired and outdated methods. So let us consign to the dustbin of history the half Nelson, the Napoleon and any other type of close that is forced, transparent, manipulative and is likely to get you thrown out!

We prefer the word commitment. Throughout the sales process, you need to ensure there is momentum and commitment to the next stage – whether that be another meeting or the final decision. When assessing the outcome of a sales call, get clear on what is an advance and what is simply a stand-still result. Many people kid themselves that 'enhancing the relationship' means it was a good call. This is not an advance. No action or next step was agreed. Ask questions such as:

'Where do we go from here?'

'*If you were in a position to work with us – when would a decision be made?*'

'*What do you want to focus on in the next meeting?*'

Thinking of the 'close' as an act that happens at the end is simplistic and unrealistic. It happens throughout the process. A Brilliant Salesperson tests for commitment through all stages of the sale and will abandon the process if there is no real interest or commitment from the other party. Of course you have to believe you can get the

> A Brilliant Salesperson tests for commitment through all stages of the sale

deal and that the deal is good for the prospect. What we are looking for here is a simple conclusion to a consultative process.

Commitment at the end can be natural because if you have done your job right – identified needs and wants, matched these with specific benefits that your product / service brings and handled objections well, then there is a good chance the buyer will buy. Make the final approach natural – people don't like being sold to. Focus on the relationship, not the close.

Ask some anticipatory questions:

'*What else do you need from us?*'

'*Do you have all the information required to make a decision?*'

'*Are we in a position to move towards discussing next steps?*'

You may have to ask for commitment, but again make it simple:

'*Are you happy to proceed now?*'

'*Have you heard enough for us to start working together?*'

'*What is the best way to move this forward now?*'

the final decision often happens without you in the room. That is fine

The reality is that the final decision often happens without you in the room. That is fine. If you have done your job well, and think what you are offering is the best, you will get the business.

 brilliant recap

In the final recap of this Part we want to remind you that:

- Traditional closing just does not work nowadays – buyers are too savvy, and it is, frankly, clunky and mechanical. Avoid the worst type of end game closing that had its day long ago!
- Customers still need to say yes, so you still need to get commitment.
- Test for commitment throughout the sales process – are they really interested?

Far from being an all or nothing last minute panic signal, getting commitment in a sale is a layered process that begins when a prospect agrees to meet you. Think of it in this way and getting commitment is something that happens in business and in life all the time.

PART 6

Developing customers

I n the 1990s, I had spent a significant amount of time developing a sales relationship with a prospect around a particular high-value product I was looking to sell. I had done everything 'by the book': I had met the decision makers and influencers, positioned the compelling benefits of our solution and our differentiator as a company and met their objections. Finally, I won the deal. It felt great and off I went to manage the rest of my pipeline. Nine months later I was called by my customer to ask if I was interested in bidding for a new project. My customer was not sure if our software would be appropriate but wanted to give us a chance. I went in full of confidence – our software did do what they wanted and the customer had a previous, positive experience of working with us. Imagine my frustration when I lost the opportunity to a major competitor. How could they? They knew we could deliver, they knew our service was great and I had a relationship with some of the main decision makers!

My lesson came when I visited my contact to get some feedback on why we had lost out. It was tough feedback to hear but it has stood me in good stead ever since. The successful competitor had done what I had done originally to get my first deal. They had taken time to meet with decision makers, they had listened to concerns, positioned specific elements of their solution that they found out were really important to the prospect and they had assumed nothing. I had made the critical mistake of believing that, just because I had invested time to understand the customer's needs around the initial opportunity, I could just pitch up and their loyalty to me would be enough to secure a project that I knew we were ideally suited for. I had assumed that, once I had secured the customer, I would naturally be at the front of their mind for future opportunities and, because of this belief, I simply focused on other prospects until the telephone rang.

Winning the initial sale is only part of the job of a Brilliant Salesperson. Relationship is not cultivated in a single sale. If you think about long-term relationships outside of work, the real challenge once you have established them is to keep them!

In the final part of this book we will answer the following questions:

- Why managing our existing customers is a great use of our time.
- What are the key priorities in managing an existing customer?
- How can I develop a relationship that erects barriers to entry by competitors?
- What activities can I engage in to 'stack the cards' in favour of continued business from my customers?

CHAPTER 26

The value of a customer

One of the things that the story in the introduction to this final part of this book really taught me was that you do not fully realise the value of having something until you lose it. Once I had secured the order that I was working on, the customer took second place to the other deals I was working on and needed to close to make my numbers. Because of this, I lost focus on maintaining and developing the relationship and this led directly to me losing possible business.

> you do not fully realise the value of having something until you lose it

There are a few things that are almost always true about a customer – someone we have sold something to at least once:

- They have invested in us as a salesperson. They have trusted us enough to buy from us.

- They have been sold on the value that we can bring them – at least around the original sale.

- They have taken us some time to develop – we have invested our time in them.

- In order to have influenced them to buy from us we probably had to build and demonstrate some level of rapport and credibility with them.

Both you and the customer have invested a lot of time and effort in getting to the point of making a sale. To some extent, there is already a positive relationship in place. But like most relationships, if you do not invest a little time in maintaining and developing them, the quality begins to suffer and, when you next want to call on it, maybe the strength of relationship is not sufficient to give you the outcome you want, maybe things have changed while you were busy on other things and other relationships.

'Treasure your relationships, not your possessions.' – Anthony J. D'Angelo

What is the cost of acquiring business?

Winning business has costs associated with it. We may not see a 'cash' value for the different steps involved but the cost is real enough. In economics there is a term called 'opportunity cost'. Simply defined, it means that putting our resources on one thing means you are foregoing using the same resource (time, for example) to achieve something else. For example, if you spend your hard-earned money on a car, that money is not now available as a deposit on a house. In sales terms, the question that it raises is: what could we have done with our time and what could it have yielded if we were not selling to this particular customer? We need

work out the cost of acquiring the business in the first place

to consider how much time and other resources we have spent securing this one customer in order to see the real value of our investment.

 brilliant exercise

Take a few minutes to try and work out the cost of acquiring the business in the first place. Whilst your sales situations may vary, consider the following table and make a guess at the time and monetary value (either by you or the company you work for) associated with each step listed:

	Time	Monetary value
Initial prospecting		
Meetings (including administration and follow-ups)		
Presentations and proposals		
Internal meetings and management of the prospect		
What is the value of missed opportunities that I could not focus on because I was spending time on this?		

Whilst this table is not 'science', it can help us see how important it is to protect the investment we have made and maximise it through maintaining and developing the relationship.

Brilliant fact

It is often five times easier to sell to an existing client than to generate a new client.

A well and proactively managed client is more likely to:

- Tell other people how pleased they are with your service levels, which may lead to new prospects.

- See you as a partner rather than a salesperson – someone not in it for a quick gain – which builds trust and loyalty, making it easier to identify and secure future sales.

- Erect barriers to entry for your competitors because of the strength of relationship that exists between you and them.

- Take less time to sell products to in the future because they know you.

'A relationship, I think, is like a shark, you know? It has to constantly move forward or it dies. And I think what we got on our hands is a dead shark.' – Woody Allen

brilliant recap

Brilliant Salespeople understand the value of a customer. In this short chapter the key points that we have focused on were:

- It is 5 times easier to secure additional work from an existing client than to win a new client.

- There is a cost in acquiring a new client and, like any other investment we make, we should protect the investment and maximise its potential.

- We need to focus time on maintaining and developing the relationship with a customer or it will die!

CHAPTER 27

Managing the 'relationship'

Having invested a lot of time in establishing a relationship with the customer that enables them to buy from us, it is important that we take time to maintain and develop the relationship if we have an interest in selling to this customer at some point in the future. For some of you, repeat purchases might represent a regular opportunity. For others, it may be that any repeat purchase is less frequent, possibly for a different product or service that you also sell (now or in the future) or for add-ons to the original sale.

Selling different products or services – possibly managed by other salespeople within your business - is called 'cross-selling' and it represents a real opportunity to extend the relationship with the customer and erect barriers to entry by a competitor by adding value in other areas of their business. Even if you are not responsible for the other product or service that can be sold you can ask the customer questions to understand their need and make an introduction to the right person. This is likely to be reciprocated so everyone wins in the long run.

Unless you have no real opportunity to sell to a customer again, managing the customer relationship is important. But how do you manage something as individual and subjective as a 'relationship'?

It is likely that a principle that works in many facets of life will also be true for you: 80% of your business will come from 20% of your customers. This Pareto Principle means we need to be clear and objective about which customers represent the real opportunity and ensure we spend adequate time developing those relationships.

'We control 50% of a relationship. We influence 100% of it.' – Anon

What relationship do we want with our customer?

It is an interesting question to consider. We often do not think about defining a relationship in specific terms but, as you are likely to get more of what you focus on, we should consider what we want before we think about how we go about getting it!

 exercise

1   Think of what an 'ideal' customer relationship would look like from **your** own perspective. Pick 5–10 words that would characterise the relationship.

2   Now put yourself **in the shoes of the customer**. From this perspective, what words would you use to describe the ideal relationship with your supplier?

To what extent do you take steps to create a relationship in line with your answer to the second question? To what extent do you think your own desired ideal relationship matches that of the customer's view?

If we think about sales relationships we have as a customer, we find that characteristics such as rapport, trust, adding value, honesty and so on are what are important to us. Any activities we engage in to manage customer relationships should, therefore, demonstrate and develop these. Alternatively, you could just ask the customer! Two great questions to find out where you need to focus your efforts are:

'What's important to you about your relationship with a supplier?'

'If I was doing a great job of managing our relationship with you, what would I be doing?'

Getting the relationship that you want

Clearly, the customer relationship is a commercial one and so it is appropriate for us to think about it in terms of what we want from it as well as from the customer's perspective.

If we are to be truly effective at managing customer relationships then we need to bear in mind the following five key points:

- Avoid making assumptions.
- Be proactive.
- Set relationship goals.
- How we move the depth and value of the relationship forward.
- How we manage difficulties when they occur.

Let us look in more detail at each of these points.

Avoid making assumptions

'Assumptions are the termites of relationships.' – Henry Winkler

Salespeople often inflate the quality of the relationship they think they have with their customers. They like to think that their customers are going to be thinking about them whenever they have an opportunity to buy another product and that the relationship that exists will prevent competitors gaining entry to the account.

When you find yourself being a little complacent about the quality, depth or breadth of your customer relationship, challenge yourself to find evidence as to why your view of the relationship is correct. Typical areas where we can make assumptions that might prove incorrect and could damage the relationship, if not checked with the customer, include:

> 80% of your business will come from 20% of your customers

- How often to contact the customer to update them or just stay in touch.

- That the customer knows what else we do and how it could help them.

- That the customer will not meet with or consider products from competitors now that we have the relationship.

- That we have demonstrated, and continue to demonstrate, sufficient 'value add' for the customer to keep considering us.

- That their situation will stay the same over time.

Be proactive

Consider for a moment a successful long-term relationship that you have with someone outside or inside of work. Do you occasionally pick up the phone to this person, think of them if you hear about something that might be of interest to them and pass it on, remember birthdays, occasionally just do something because you know they will appreciate it?

Very few long-term relationships have survived without some effort. We need to work at them and that means being proactive. You see, relationship management is an important but not urgent task. It is one of those things that will not cause your business to fail tomorrow if you do not do it. By the time it becomes urgent it will be too late.

If you think about your approach before you won the business and secured a client you might characterise it as being 'hungry'. You demonstrated an interest and willingness to go the extra mile to secure a deal. You put effort in. Well, guess what, that is what your competitors are trying to do now with your customer!

Salespeople are sometimes characterised as either 'hunters' or 'farmers'. The hunters are those that live for the thrill of the sale. They like taking a prospect through to becoming a customer. They enjoy opening new accounts. The farmers enjoy cultivating the relationship. They are happy to sow seeds knowing that they may take a while to come to anything. If repeat or additional sales to a customer are an opportunity, you need to be able to do both. Six years ago I won a small piece of work with the UK arm of an international corporation. I focused on doing a great job and on developing a relationship with the key decision maker. I would keep them informed of things that I thought would be of interest, I put them in touch with people where I thought there could be benefit for both parties. Last year this customer represented 10% of our business.

Some examples of being proactive in managing a customer relationship include:

- Forwarding useful articles or information that you come across and think might be of value to them.
- Making introductions that might be beneficial to your customer.
- Checking how things are going with the product / service they bought from you.
- Seeking ways to develop additional contacts within the same customer.
- Meeting up less formally to find out what is current, what has changed, what the priorities are for your customer.

Set relationship goals

The only thing that is consistent about all relationships is that they are all different! No two customer relationships will be identical because they involve different personalities, cultures and situations. If we are to effectively manage relationships we need first

> We need to set relationship goals

to understand where we are now with this individual relationship and then define where we want it to be, specifically. We need to set relationship goals.

The challenge here is that relationships are subjective things and goals need to be objective. The key to making relationship goals more objective is to look for evidence of success. An important question to help is 'When I have achieved this relationship goal, how will I know?' An example will help. Let us say that you wish to develop more trust. You first need to consider how you would know if the desired level of trust existed. It may be that your customer would introduce you to his manager so you can present how you can help the business in another area, they would give you information that would help position your proposal more effectively and they would act as a telephone reference for one of your prospects. If this is the evidence that you would see, you can then start to create an action plan that would help you achieve the goal.

brilliant exercise

Pick one of your customers and consider the relationship that exists. How would you like to develop the relationship?

Ask yourself how you would know when this relationship goal was achieved – how would the achievement be evidenced either in terms of what you would see or what would happen as a result?

Set some goals based on achieving the 'evidence'. Make the goals specific, measurable and set a date for their achievement.

> We might well have tangible revenue goals for future business through this customer

Goals do not need to be limited to the relationship itself, of course. We might well have tangible revenue goals for future business through this customer.

How we move the depth and value of the relationship forward

Setting specific goals is important if we are to move the relationship forward, but it helps to have some context for these goals; some sense of the relationship 'journey' that we are looking to take our client on. If we can increase the depth of relationship we have with customers we are erecting barriers for competitors and increasing our chances of additional sales going forward.

One model that is widely used is to consider different levels of relationship that exist. This can help us consider our priorities and the actions we need to take generically to help move customer relationships forward. Often, specific definitions depend on your company, context and customers but the following provides an illustration of how this approach can work.

The start point is objectivity. We need to define the different relationship 'levels' that could exist and what, specifically, characterises them. We may have the following definitions:

Level	Definition
Prospect	Someone who has not yet bought from us but is a qualified potential customer.
Customer	Someone who has bought from us once. They may or may not have any loyalty to us.
Client	Someone who has bought from us more than once. They have demonstrated that they see the value we offer.
Supporter	Someone who acts as a reference for us. We have relationships with all of the key decision makers and 70%+ of the influencers.
Advocate	We have a close relationship at senior management and middle management levels. We know all of the decision makers and influencers. We share strategic plans and the customer inputs ideas and suggestions into our product development.

As you move from prospect to advocate you are increasing the depth and quality of the relationship that exists. This makes it much more difficult for competitors to get in the door.

Getting the relationship that you want!

---

brilliant exercise

Consider what levels of relationship would be appropriate and desirable in your context.

How would you define them?

Now classify your existing customers into these levels – be objective!

Defining relationship levels enables you to then ask the question: 'What do I need to do to move a Client to a Supporter?' for example. This will give rise to some specific actions that you can take.

How we manage difficulties when they occur

'Even the best of friends face conflicts, but that needn't mean the end of the relationship.' – Anon

In most long-term relationships, problems or difficulties occur. It is just a fact of life and sales is no different. Difficulties come in many forms, big and small, and examples in sales include:

- Late delivery to our customer.
- Having a particularly aggressive negotiation over terms.
- Giving the customer incorrect information by mistake.
- Not following through on a commitment we made.

Whilst we do what we can to avoid difficulties occurring, what separates Brilliant Salespeople from the rest is how they respond to and manage difficulties when they do, inevitably, arise. A difficulty can be defined as anything that can disrupt the relationship that we have. In itself, it could be a small thing; something that is not, on its own, enough to create a big problem. The problem is that if we ignore enough of the small things by brushing them under the carpet or giving a response to the customer which does not truly satisfy them, then the next 'small' thing could be the 'straw that breaks the camel's back'.

These small, individual difficulties are called pinches. If we ignore them and do not address the difficulty appropriately then, over time, each of these pinches build up on top of

> small, individual difficulties are called pinches

one another and can seriously damage the relationship. It could end in 'crunch' time. The danger is that any one of these small difficulties might not seem too important to us and, indeed, in isolation it may not be. We need to manage relationships proactively and in a timely way. Doing this will build a stronger and more trusting relationship.

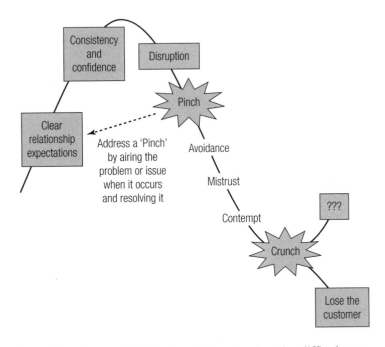

One thing that can hold us back from 'having the difficult conversation' is that we do not know how to approach the conversation and we are fearful of the possible reaction. It is best, however, to address difficulties honestly when they occur. You can always say something like the following:

'I have just realised that I gave you some information that was incorrect and, because our relationship with you is important, I wanted to put it right.'

'As I think back to our negotiation last week I am concerned that I might have been too aggressive and I want to talk about it so that it does not negatively impact our relationship.'

There is no substitute for being honest!

brilliant exercise

Consider your customer relationships and the situations that can arise where a problem, or 'pinch', could occur. Complete the following table:

Possible problem or 'pinch' point	What can I do to prevent it occurring?	What can I do to solve it appropriately if it does occur?

brilliant recap

Managing the customer relationship is critical if we are to secure more business from a customer in the future.

- Before we can manage a relationship we need to define, specifically, what relationship we want with our customers.
- We must avoid making assumptions about the relationship that exists – we need to be objective about where we are right now with the customer.
- Relationship management is an important (not urgent) task and we need to be proactive.
- Setting objective goals for the relationship is critical to moving it forward.
- Increasing the quality and depth of the relationship is an effective way of building barriers to competitors within our customers.
- We need to deal appropriately with difficulties in a relationship to avoid these 'stacking up' and damaging the relationship.

CHAPTER 28

Your priorities in managing customers

We have talked in the previous chapter about the need to take proactive action to develop customer relationships and the principles of being proactive, setting relationship goals and considering different relationship levels. But what are some of our tactical priorities in managing our customers? What are some of the things that we can do quickly and easily? How does managing our customers differ from managing relationships?

Before we give you some of our ideas, think about your own experience.

⌐ brilliant exercise

Think of times when you have bought something and been delighted by the 'customer experience'. You were made to feel special or, at the very least, the salesperson was focused on relationship rather than simply the product sale.

What did they do that made you feel special or that there was a focus on relationship?

How, specifically, did it make you feel?

It is difficult to separate the idea of managing customers from managing relationship, as the two are so closely linked. Most good customer management benefits the relationship, and vice versa. Our priorities in managing customers are quite simple but are often not done by salespeople. Whatever our own motivation we need to think about customer management from the perspective of what our customer wants from us.

'A customer is the most important visitor on our premises; he is not dependent on us. We are dependent on him. He is not an interruption in our work. He is the purpose of it. He is not an outsider in our business. He is part of it. We are not doing him a favor by serving him. He is doing us a favor by giving us an opportunity to do so.' – Mahatma Gandhi

Managing our customers starts from the moment that we get the order, but there are different 'categories' that our activities can be divided into. This chapter looks at each of the main categories of activity and gives you some top tips and priorities for each one.

Using the customer as a resource

A customer is a valuable resource to us, and not just because they have paid for a product or service that we have provided. We can utilise their decision to purchase in a number of ways to help us increase our business. As part of our management of the customer we need to consider how we can maximise the benefit of their becoming a customer of ours.

A customer can:

- Act as a reference: either with a written testimonial or on the telephone with prospects.
- Be the subject of a case study: we can use case studies as marketing and sales collateral and to help other prospects in a similar situation understand the real benefits of working with our product / service and with us as a company.

- Give us referrals to other potential customers: your customer probably knows other people who could benefit from your product or service and can give you their names.

Interestingly, asking customers to act as a reference or give you referrals actually increases their sense of loyalty towards you as a supplier. By agreeing to do either of these things, the customer is 'putting their name' to your product and company. This makes them more likely to tell others about it and to speak positively about you (as long as you give a good service and your product does what it says!).

> The time to ask for referrals is at the peak of the customer's gratitude curve

When should you ask?

There is something called a 'gratitude curve' and the time to ask for referrals is when your customer is at the peak of their gratitude curve. This might be at the time of purchase by the customer or, if your product delivers value after a period of time, it might be at the point that the customer realises the value, so you need to think about it. For example, I had an amazing meal recently that was at a table situated in the middle of the kitchen of the restaurant. It was eight courses, and you interacted with the Chef. At the point when I had finished the meal, would I have been prepared to write a brief testimonial or tell my friends? Absolutely!

When we have delivered some training or consulting work that has made a positive difference to the customer we have a habit of asking for the names of two or three people that we might contact and introduce our services to, mentioning their name as an existing customer. If you do a good job, people will be pleased to give you names.

brilliant tips

> 1 Identify, for your product or service, when the customer is likely to be at the peak of their gratitude curve.
>
> 2 List all of the ways in which you could utilise this.

Adding value to the customer – constantly

We work with someone called Ed Stivala on our website and internet-related work, and from the moment we met him he was looking for ways to add value to our business. This does not mean that he tries to sell us on new products he has or more consultancy. In fact, it is quite the reverse: he focuses on looking for how he can help our business in any way possible and this might be through a suggestion, an introduction to someone or even challenging our thinking and helping us see that we might be wrong! You can see some of his work at www.brilliant-selling.com

'We see our customers as invited guests to a party, and we are the hosts. It's our job every day to make every important aspect of the customer experience a little bit better.' – Jeff Bezo

> By adding value whenever you can, you build trust

By adding value whenever you can, you build trust. Here are seven ways in which you can add value. They are just examples:

- Send information that allows them to be better educated about their market – press cuttings, latest research, the competition to their company.
- Demonstrate how they can make more money in a new way.
- Demonstrate how they can save money.
- Send something for free which may have a high perceived value.
- Think about educating them in every face-to-face meeting.

- Offer training to the staff.
- Invite them to a networking event.

And if you want to know what you could do that would **really** add value to the customer, you could just ask: 'What could I do that would add most value going forward?'

Customer knowledge and understanding

Part of our ongoing management of our customers has to be to get as clear a picture as possible of their organisation as it relates to our product or service offering.

- Understand the challenges and priorities they face in their market.
- Broaden our contact base within the customer – identify decision makers and influencers, get introductions to them.
- Understand the culture and how decisions are made.
- Understand the personal wins and motivations for the key contacts we have.
- Find out what is happening in the business that might represent more opportunity for us.
- Research them using tools such as the internet so that we are aware of changes that could help or hinder us, and can be proactive in adding value through our business-focused conversations with them.

brilliant tip

One of the easiest and most effective ways of increasing customer knowledge and understanding is by spending time with the customer. Look for opportunities – formally and socially if appropriate – to meet and ask questions.

General good practice

Here are some general 'good practice' tips. Most take very little time to do and have a disproportionate benefit. All of these are proactive and important (never urgent) tasks, and so the challenge is for you to make the time to do them.

Welcome new customers

Get the relationship off to a good start by formally welcoming the customer where appropriate. This might be with a small welcome gift, a letter outlining your commitment or something else that makes them feel valued. And, no, this is not the same as sending your standard terms and conditions of sale! To find out more about welcome packs, read the article contained in the free resource pack that accompanies this book (email **resources@brilliant-selling.com** to receive this pack).

Expectations meetings

Once a contract has been signed, and especially where you will be interacting a lot with the customer around the delivery of the product or service, it is often beneficial to have an expectations meeting. The details of a working relationship between customer and supplier are often not discussed explicitly and this makes it more likely for one or other party to not meet the other's expectations. Having an explicit conversation around how the relationship and interaction will work is well suited to a consultative sales approach and can head off possible difficulties before they occur. Also, once you have had a conversation about, for example, how quickly you will respond to telephone messages, it makes it easier to refer to these agreed standards and expectations when a difficulty does arise.

Examples of topics to include in an expectations meeting are:

● How we will communicate – how often, telephone, face-to-face, etc.

● Agreeing to raise problems immediately they occur.

- What we will deliver, specifically.
- What we need from you, specifically.
- Agreement to review how the relationship is going.

Immediate follow-up

Get into the habit of following up meetings or telephone calls immediately. The follow-up could be as simple as confirming a meeting and outline agenda following a telephone call or emailing the customer your understanding of the actions and timescales following a meeting you attended.

Account planning

The specifics of this will vary widely depending on your circumstances, but it is always good practice to have a plan. Without an account plan you lack direction and focus. If you need to interact with other people in your company in order to sell, then a clear plan helps them see where you are headed and their part in the bigger picture.

At its most basic, an account plan needs to consider what your goal is with the customer over what period of time, along with the key actions that you need to take. More comprehensive account plans might include information about the following:

- Contact details for influencers and decision makers in the account.
- How each of them feel about your company.
- Individual action plans to influence decision makers.
- Information about the client and their priorities and challenges.

tip

The free resource pack accompanying this book contains examples of account planning templates to give you ideas of what you need to focus on. Email **resources@brilliant-selling.com** to receive your copy.

Staying in touch

Although it is good common sense to stay in touch with your customers, we often do not do this as regularly as we should. As long as the relationship is built on us adding value, the customer is unlikely to object to staying in touch and it is important that our customers know that we are thinking of them. There are a number of ways of doing this other than the 'I'm just calling to stay in touch' approach. Here are ten ways you can stay in touch with your customers.

- Send them a newsletter.
- Have formal meetings.
- Invite them for a drink or to a social or corporate event.
- Invite them to a networking opportunity.
- Give them a call on the telephone ('I just saw something in this month's ... and thought you might be interested...').
- Send magazine or web articles that might be of value or interest to them.
- Send them a birthday card.
- Inform them of changes in policy or management.
- Give them an opportunity to meet your boss.
- Call them to make sure they received the order, find out what they thought.

Meeting management

Meetings represent a significant investment in your time (especially if you have to travel to the customer) and we must take responsibility for making the most of this investment by following some simple but important points:

- When you arrange a meeting, make sure you propose an agenda and give the customer an opportunity to comment on it. This shows you are interested, professional and keen to maximise the use of time.

- Always confirm a meeting by email – especially if it has been arranged a long time in advance.

- Think about ways in which you can add value in every meeting.

- When the meeting starts, clarify that the agenda is still appropriate and the amount of time you have for the meeting.

- Be clear on the desired outcome or objective for a meeting. This focuses the participants on achieving it and helps prevent a meeting drifting off track.

- Summarise the actions, responsibilities and timelines at the end of the meeting and confirm by email.

brilliant recap

Managing our customers effectively need not take up lots of time. There are some priorities and in this section we have focused on the following key points:

- Always consider how we can utilise the customer as a resource through referrals, references and case studies.
- Constantly look for ways to add value to the customer.
- Take time to increase your knowledge of the customer, their issues and your contacts within the company.
- Make sure you stay in touch with your customers.

Have a plan for the customer – know where you want to get to with them!

Summary
– your brilliant future

It has been quite a journey!

You may have read the whole book (if so, we are impressed with your dedication) or you may have dipped into sections which we hope have offered new insights. Reading this book may have stimulated your thinking about how to sell Brilliantly. We are at the end point. However, your learning journey may have only just begun! We have told you what we think, we have asked you to get involved, we have focused on the practicalities of selling and now it is over to you again. Are you someone with good intentions or do you take action when you know it makes sense?

Most of you will have been on a training course at some point in your career and will be familiar with the typical ending – creating an action plan. The truth is that without positive action this book will soon become a distant memory (only after, of course, you have told all your friends about it).

'If you always do what you've always done, you'll always get what you always got' – NLP presupposition

Do you want to get even better results? Do you understand the importance of executing on new ideas as soon as possible? If so, take some time to reflect now …

Below is a reminder of what we have covered. As you look back now on the content of Brilliant Selling, identify the three core areas on which you want to focus.

Here is a reminder of what we have covered:

Part 1: You

- The personality of a salesperson.
- How values and beliefs impact sales success.
- Performance and selling.
- Continually improve through self-coaching.

Part 2: Process and planning

- The sales process as a tool for improvement.
- Making the most of your time.
- Planning for success.
- Setting the right goals.
- Managing sales information.

Part 3: Your power to influence

- Credibility and rapport – the foundations of effective influencing.
- Managing your state – being confident whenever you want.
- Asking the right questions.
- Listening and learning.
- Negotiating collaboratively.

Part 4: Understanding buyers and prospects

- How do you sell?
- The modern buyer.
- Prospecting with purpose.
- Initial meeting(s) with prospect.
- Identifying what the prospect wants and needs.

Part 5: Presenting solutions

- Appealing to the customer.
- Writing great sales proposals.

- Preparing winning pitches.
- Persuasive delivery.
- Making the most of objections.
- Closing and commitment.

Part 6: Developing customers

- The value of a customer.
- Managing the 'relationship'.
- Your priorities in managing customers.

Grab a pen right now and answer these questions for each of the three areas you have nominated:

- What in particular did you find useful about this part?
- How can you start applying these learning points to your current role?
- What are you going to do in the next four weeks?
- What are you going to do tomorrow?
- How will you know you have made the changes you want to make?

Go out there and make a difference. If you need more support then visit us at **www.brilliant-selling.com**. If you want to look at our sales resource library then email us RIGHT NOW at **resources@brilliant-selling.com**. Enjoy the ride – you have what it takes to be a Brilliant Salesperson!

And finally a story …

Some years ago now, there lived an ambitious young artist. He lived in a small village on the edge of a narrow valley. Often, he would gather his materials up and clamber to the top of the nearest hill and, from the shade of a large oak tree, he surveyed all that was in front of him. He spent hours up there, under the same comfortable tree, painting and contemplating. He thought about who he was and what he could become. He practised painting – in oil, water colour and pencil. He worked hard to notice the shape and outline of his village in different lights as the seasons changed inexorably around him. He found that the more he practised, the better he got. He noticed that if he took the time to plan his vision in detail, the pictures were richer and more evocative.

Word soon spread and within a few short years he had a strong following in the local community. He cultivated good relations with all who were interested in his work, and he became celebrated as an expert on the local landscape. He began to make good money from his work and noticed that the better he became, the less he had to bargain. He was delighted that some of his patrons wanted to buy more of his work, and he listened carefully and asked questions to discover what they particularly had in mind.

He began to exhibit his work in a local gallery and was careful to create a special space so that his paintings were shown at their best. Locals and many others, from further afield, came and were impressed with his versatility and craftsmanship and the careful and subtle way he framed his pictures.

One beautiful autumn day some years later, when the shade from the oak tree that sheltered his position on the hillside was lengthening, and he was finishing a commission, he thought about what he wanted to do next. He was restless. He knew in his heart of hearts that to improve as an artist he would have to leave the safety of the valley and expand his horizons. He resolved that this was the next stage in his journey. So the very next day, having thanked his patrons, and promising to keep in touch, he set off for the next valley and the valley beyond. Over the years, he continued to improve and his skills were noticed by more and more people. As he travelled, the richness of his paintings was matched by the wealth in his pocket. But he always remembered that his artistic journey started in a small village on the edge of a narrow valley, under the shade of that old oak tree.